DO THE UNRIGHT THING:

MEMOIR OF A PEOPLE PLEASER

DO THE UNRIGHT THING:

MEMOIR OF A PEOPLE PLEASER

STEVE FREDLUND

MANUSCRIPTS
PRESS

DO THE UNRIGHT THING:
Memoir of a People Pleaser

ISBN 979-8-88926-857-4 *Paperback*

979-8-88926-858-1 *Hardcover*

979-8-88926-856-7 *Digital Ebook*

This book is dedicated to my mother, Ellen Lance,
who always encouraged my quirky creativity as a young boy
and fought for my happiness as I grew up.
You continue to be an example of living a life of love and
laughter, even when I beat you in our morning puzzles.

"Don't ask yourself what the world needs. Ask yourself what makes you come alive, and go do that, because what the world needs is people who have come alive."

—HOWARD THURMAN

CONTENTS

CONTENTS

AUTHOR'S NOTE

Thank you so much for reading *Do the Unright Thing: Memoir of a People Pleaser.*

No matter what struggle we have in our lives, those who don't get it, don't get it. But those who have been there, or are there, find great comfort in talking with others who also get it. That is why I have written this book. Sure, I have found the process of writing it to be personally cathartic, but the reason it is published is to serve as a comfort, if not a resource, to others who understand the oppressive pressure of trying to do everything right and meet every expectation.

I always thought it was so cliché for a speaker or author to say, "I felt so alone," or, "I didn't think anyone would understand what I was going through." Like any good, logical person would do, I rolled my eyes and made a "pfft" noise, or maybe even said sarcastically under my breath, "Okay, here we go."

But then it happened to me—that feeling like no one would understand what I was going through. My people-pleasing actions as a young boy gave way to a full-on dependence on external validation, allowing others to define how to live my life as I focused on satisfying their expectations. Surely, I thought, no one else could relate to this. However, as I started sharing my story, others shared theirs, revealing how many of us have been trapped in a life of trying so hard to do everything right, as defined by others.

I am not encouraging you to do the wrong thing. I am inviting you to do the thing that is right for you, even if it is unright in the eyes of your family, friends, boss, or social media. Even when I realized my dependence on validation, it took many years to summon the courage to do my first unright thing. The empowerment I felt in taking that first step gave me more courage for the next one, and the next, and the next.

Eventually, I did so many unright things, they led me to my right thing, becoming a professional speaker. Known as "The Safari Dude," I make five invitations (the Big Five) to my audiences to help them become happier in life, work, and leadership: Choose your experience, do the unright thing, get the right peeps in your Jeep, take in the view, and embrace the adventure. These five key things also lead to having a truly epic African safari.

If you would like to find out more about me or my keynote speaking, please go to SteveFredlund.com and shoot me an email or give me a call.

CHAPTER 1:

THE ADVENTURES
OF STAT MAN

Sometimes passion runs so deep it tells a story about who we are and what is truly important to us. For me, it was hard to find places where I felt free to be completely myself and express my authentic passion.

This is why, when I was young, I loved going to my grandparents' farm outside Milaca, Minnesota. It was a rare break from chronically feeling "out of place." Their couch was a welcomed friend, one where I felt safe from judgment. It seemed by its very sturdy nature to protect me from the embarrassment of feeling weird or oddly quirky. Its deeply colored fabric also protected my history by concealing Kool-Aid spills and food stains.

As a thirteen-year-old, visiting the farm was magical: the cows, the crops, working on jigsaw puzzles, and the pajamas grandma had for us that held so much static we created lightning shows under the covers at night. My brother, Larry, and I liked to run around outside, exploring to see if grandpa dumped anything new behind the barns or trying to set a record for how far we could travel on the hay bales without our feet touching the ground. I loved these adventures, but some days Larry had to be a solo explorer. No matter how much he begged, how gorgeous it was outside, or even if a bull got loose from his pen, when it was an October Saturday on the farm, I would be watching college football.

I lay on my stomach with my head about a foot away from Grandma's thirteen-inch color television. I was close enough to reach the rabbit ear antennas when things got a little fuzzy, and I had to hold the dial somewhere between channels four and five when the big squiggles came on the screen.

This day was a big day for college football fans like me, starting with Ohio State and Oklahoma, two absolute juggernauts with larger-than-life coaches Earle Bruce and Barry Switzer. Announcing the game was a hero of mine, the incomparable Keith Jackson, whose memorable calls would give me shivers for the next forty years. I wanted to freeze time. Grandma brought me peanuts in the shell and didn't seem to care that I made a big mess as I attacked them like the squirrels outside her window. Grandpa spent his breaks from chores taking naps in his chair behind me. I was usually so concerned that everyone else was happy, but here I was oblivious to anything outside the magic thirteen-inch box that teleported me to college campuses around the country.

I was daydreaming about being in the stadium, not just as a fan but as a student. In my head I pretended and believed this was *my* school, and this was *my* team playing today. I visualized I was wearing *my* school colors and had my face painted too. I was cheering at the top of my lungs with my fellow classmates rooting for our team. The pep band, cheerleaders... all of us there together focused and passionate about one thing. Our cheering turned to a roar as our team ran through the tunnel and onto the field. Our school song came on, and we raised our voices as one. I could see it like it was happening, and I could feel I belonged.

Grandma returned from her rhubarb patch, her soft humming interrupting my daydream, but I didn't mind. Grandma lovingly shared, "Your Uncle Steve is coming later to watch the Gopher game with you." I was ecstatic! I loved Uncle Steve, not just because I was named after him but because he was so cool.

He was in his twenties and an engineer working at a large company in the Twin Cities, and he also loved football. We were alike in many ways, and he always seemed to get me, which was something I longed for, especially being a new teenager. From my youthful eyes, his life seemed epic. I also knew he respected and cared about me, and that meant a lot. Sometimes he brought a frozen pizza for us to share as we watched the game. I loved this rare and special treat!

The front door opened, and it was him. There was a commercial, so without a thought I ran to hug him. He smiled with a wide grin. He always made me feel truly accepted. He handed something to Grandma, and I fought the urge to ask him if he brought a frozen pizza, but of course I hoped he did.

He turned to go back out to his car, but he knew I hated missing even a single play, so told me, "You better get back in there so you don't miss anything!" I reached the TV just as the commercials ended.

Now that Uncle Steve was there, I decided to sit on the couch so there'd be plenty of room for him, too, and I was not lying down like a child. It was a great game, and I couldn't wait for the next commercial break to tell him about it.

Uncle Steve sat next to me and handed me something, giving me a big smile. "This is for you." It was a T-shirt from Texas Instruments, the company he worked for. I felt like the most important person in the world, being given a gift by someone I admired so much. Then he asked, "So, what's happening in the game?"

I updated him on Ohio State and Oklahoma and some of the other scores from the top twenty games around the country. We both thought the Gophers didn't have much of a shot against Nebraska, but we agreed you never knew. He asked me questions about my life as if I was an adult and then thoughtfully listened to my answers and asked follow-up questions. Uncle Steve really got me.

Kickoff for the Gopher game was right around the corner as he made his way to the kitchen after casually mentioning he would be right back. A few moments later I heard the unmistakable click and whoosh of Grandma's gas stove. He peeked around the corner, showing just a piece of red and black box. "How does this sound?" he asked knowing fully how I would respond. How could this day get any better? Maybe with a major Gopher upset.

To our great disappointment Nebraska gave our Gophers a world-class whooping, eighty-four to thirteen, in one of the worst losses in college football history. Like true Minnesotans, my Uncle Steve and I looked for bright spots and moral victories. "It could have been worse." "The offense looked pretty good."

The positives were hard to find as the announcers went through the final stats, explaining how Nebraska racked up nearly eight hundred yards of offense and another two hundred in kick returns as they scored twenty-one points every quarter. Uncle Steve and I broke down the stats even further in our post-game analysis.

I knew it was just a pipe dream to one day be in a college stadium like that myself, but watching football on the farm brought me into the action of these games like nowhere else. No one at my house was a football fan and certainly couldn't understand my complete obsession with the game and the entire college football experience. During my classes at school, I caught myself humming fight songs of Notre Dame, Ohio State, USC, and Alabama. I probably knew the Michigan fight song better than most of their alumni.

On rare occasions I could watch the Gophers on TV at home, but I was just as happy listening to the games on the radio and keeping my own stats in real time. I did this for both the University of Minnesota football and basketball games. I had notebooks filled with individual game and season-long statistics. One of my heroes was Ray Christensen, the iconic play-by-play announcer for the Gophers. Sometimes I imagined meeting him and dreamt he loved how passionate I was while also thinking I was cool.

To me Ray had the most amazing job: watching football games and sharing his thoughts with the world as it was happening. I would've been thrilled to do something like that too.

I was only thirteen at the time, but I already felt like a long-suffering Minnesota sports fan. Like every other football season I've experienced, this one ended with disappointment. The Gophers won only one game, and the Vikings missed the playoffs. It seemed cruel our harsh winters happened right as our football teams were closing another disappointing year.

I didn't like the cold, but winters had been a bit more bearable the past few years ever since I turned nine when my mom remarried. Her husband, Doug, adopted me and my brother, changing our last name from Rice to Fredlund. Doug owned two old snowmobiles that Larry and I were allowed to use, even though they broke down a bit too often.

With Doug came a new extended family, where, at first, I felt like an outsider. However, that was about to change. The summer between middle and high school we had attended a picnic with Doug's family. My new Uncle Donn approached me, and at first, I thought I was going to get in trouble for drinking too much of the green sugary sherbet punch.

Instead, Donn said, "I hear you are a football fan."

I nodded as my eyes focused on him. I could tell I had green remnants on my lips, so I wiped them away with the back of my hand. I knew I should have taken a napkin.

"Your mom also tells me you are pretty good at keeping stats." I tried to verbalize an answer, but nodding was the best I could do. "I need your help. I do the play-by-play for the Cambridge Bluejackets football games on the radio, and it's too hard to do that while keeping all the stats. Do you think you could help me?"

I think I blacked out momentarily before responding, maybe a little too loudly, "You mean, you do play-by-play like Ray Christensen?"

I didn't realize how great my new Uncle Donn's laugh was, even though at first it startled me. "Well, I guess so! I'm not as good as Ray, but I suppose that is correct. He has a full team of people to help him with stats, but I just need one, and I choose you. Are you interested?"

Here was a person who valued that I kept stats on all the games and didn't think it was weird at all. I held back tears by the time the words formulated. "I would love that." His smile invited me to share more. "I have stats from every game if you need to see them. I can show you how I do it. Should I bring some to your house?" It didn't seem like he should just offer this to me without seeing if I was good enough for what he needed.

"That's not necessary, Steve. You got the job. We have a couple of months before the season starts, and we will figure it all out then. Also, have you heard about the Prep Bowl?"

I was so focused on wanting to know what I needed to prepare to be his stats guy, I barely processed this second question. "Um, no."

"Now that they built the Metrodome in Minneapolis, they hold all five of the state championship football games there, and they are all on the same day. Would you like to join me next year? "

"Yes, yes! Well, let me ask my mom, but yes. That sounds amazing!"

For the next two years, I was Uncle Donn's right-hand man as he did the play-by-play for the Cambridge football and basketball games. He even let me share the stats on air a couple of times. We went to two Prep Bowls together, talking about the intricacies of football strategy. No one understood my passion for football like my new Uncle Donn, who even encouraged me to become a sports agent when I got older. He believed there was going to be a lot of money in it, and the best agents were great at numbers as well as understanding the nuances of the sport, just like I did.

It was easy to let my lack of confidence immediately dismiss what he said. It was much easier to believe something like being a sports agent was for people who were a lot smarter and more important than me.

Those autumn Saturdays at the farm and keeping stats for Uncle Donn came to an end as I got busier with high school's demands like driving, activities, and girls. Well, two out of three were true.

Uncle Steve moved to Texas, and my biological dad let my brother and me know he no longer wanted to see us. Both were tough, but I would be okay. I am certain things like this affect us more deeply than we realize, and we just can't see it until the impact shows itself.

This also seemed like the right time to scale back doing my own stats for the Gopher games on the radio. It was really kind of silly anyway. No one else I knew was doing this, and there was no future in it. The Gophers already had a play-by-play guy and a stats team.

Without Uncle Donn, Uncle Steve, Ray, or anyone else telling me otherwise, the only logical conclusion was that no sixteen-year-old should be wasting time listening to a football game on the radio and writing down how many yards each player gained, especially one who wanted to someday have a girlfriend. I was never going to find someone who thought my dozens of notebooks filled with stats was very sexy. The right thing to do was to move on from this quirky pursuit of my childhood.

But no matter what I changed, I still got goosebumps thinking about what it must feel like to attend a game at Ohio State's horseshoe stadium or Michigan's Big House; to be one of the hundred thousand people all wearing the same color and going nuts together at the game—a sense of true belonging. Maybe it was okay to hold on to these dreams for a little bit longer.

CHAPTER 2:

HOW "WEIRD AL"
MADE ME TRAP GOPHERS

———

It probably would have been better for the rest of the world if my mom hadn't let me use TV commercial jingles to answer her questions. We both thought it was funny to use songs this way, and her laughter felt pleasing inside and gave me more confidence to act on my creativity. No one was safe from my savvy spontaneous jingles. Friends would ask for gum and get the Big Red song as I gave them a piece. Mom would ask for a little break before playing a game when she got home from work, and I would respond with the Kit Kat jingle. Whatever you do, don't ask me for bologna or you will have the Oscar Mayer ditty running through your head all day.

I've always found something mysterious about how certain combinations of words and lyrics could evoke laughter, and if I was able to make someone laugh, that was the ultimate validation. I mean, who doesn't want people around who will make them laugh? I learned early on if you are funny, people like you and will speak well about you to their friends. They may even remember the funny thing you said as they pass you in the hallway and then flash you a smile. Nothing made me feel like I belonged more than the hallway smile.

Throughout middle school and high school, I used humor as my superpower to gain acceptance, which made me feel like I was okay. Maybe some people truly liked me, but that was never the goal. I just wanted to *feel* like I was okay, which meant at least they didn't *not* like me.

I put a lot of effort and time into memorizing new jokes so I could continue to feel accepted. It was my way to fit in, just like how college football helped me fit into my new family. I wanted to use my jokes to leave people wanting more, which meant they would want more of me.

I was hungry for comedic inspiration. So I had been doing odd jobs to gain the quarters and dollars needed for the latest "Weird Al" Yankovic cassette. I was almost to the amount needed on the day I broke from my usual saunter between the school bus and our house. On this day, I would collect the dollar needed to seal the deal and get the cassette.

I sprinted down the long driveway, threw my backpack on my bed, and ran back outside to hop on my bike. The road was my enemy, but its deep sand was no match for me. On this day, I would overcome every obstacle to keep moving forward. As I moved from loose sand to hard-packed gravel, the pedals became a rhythm perfectly matching the song I began belting out, Animotion's "Obsession." I changed the lyrics slightly to match my cassette commitment.

We considered anyone within a mile to be our neighbors. This included Tom and Ellie, who had been neighbors for many years. Mom and Ellie were best pals, often getting together to play cards, drink wine, and watch the Minnesota

Twins. Every time I turned into their driveway, I was overwhelmed by their huge yard, wondering how long it must take to mow. But I was sure Tom took his time because he seemed to really enjoy a good-looking lawn. I assumed that's why he offered to pay me to get rid of the gophers that infested his yard. That year he was determined to win the battle and had enlisted me to do the dirty work.

My trapping strategy was quite detailed and efficient in terms of where my twelve traps were set, the order in how they were checked, and the days and times I set them. I bought most of the traps myself, so I calculated the optimal number to give me the highest expected return on investment.

Barely into their driveway, I took a sharp left and jumped off my bike in the far southeast corner of their property. I pulled the chain on the first trap to see if there was any resistance. *Shoot, nothing!* I desperately worked my way through the trap line, pleading with the universe that today might be the day.

My walk to trap number five was a bit treacherous, so I kept my head down to make sure I didn't twist an ankle. Trap five had some activity, and my heart leapt. The cardboard was shifted, and some fresh dirt had been thrown out of the hole. I was no longer worried about twisting an ankle as I sprinted the remaining twenty feet and slid toward the trap on my knees. *Success!*

For every gopher I caught, Tom gave me a dollar, and this would give me the seven bucks I needed to make my purchase. I couldn't help but sing my victory tune all the way to their front door, a parody of "Islands in the Stream" called "Gophers in the Trap." Sometimes I imagined holding it out in front of the crowd at the Rose Bowl who would sing my song in unison, clapping their hands together every time the song got to the word "trap."

Tom saw me coming and had my dollar ready for me. "Way to go, Steve." I took a moment to let the validation soak in. He was a big city police officer, so a congratulations from him was no small potatoes.

I didn't even take the time to reset trap number five or check the others. I was back on my bike and headed into town. I remembered to put the other six dollars in my pocket so I didn't have to go back home first. Again, music filled my brain and came out my mouth, this time a parody of the Eurythmics, "I travel Cambridge and Isanti County. This cool cat is looking for something."

Finally, I was there after making record time. I laid my bike on the ground, reminding myself to fix the kickstand. Sweat was pouring from my head as I walked into Pamida, our local shopping center. I made my usual grand entrance into the store, giving a smile to Peg who was in her usual spot behind the counter. I started singing one of my favorite songs, "Pa-mi-da," to the tune of "Elvira" by the Oak Ridge Boys. I sang quietly enough to not be annoying but loudly enough that maybe someone listening might take note of my natural talent.

I half-jogged past her. "Do you have any Weird Al tapes left?" She had no chance at understanding what I was saying, but it was rhetorical anyway since I knew right where she kept them. Every time I came to town, I checked out the stash, always surprised there were any left. It'd been a long three months of waiting.

My shoes were still covered in dirt, and I saw the trail I had left behind. I felt bad and decided I would offer to sweep after I made my purchase. I turned down the third aisle with the eagerness of Christmas morning. *Yes!* They were not sold out. In fact, it didn't seem like any had been bought recently.

I grabbed one of the cassette tapes and ran it to the counter as I pulled the seven dollars out of my pocket. My arms and hands were filthy as I set the cassette and money on the counter. "I'm sorry about the dirt, Peg." I should have turned on Tom's hose and washed my hands. I didn't want Peg to not like me or to tell her friends or my mom what a mess I made. "I can sweep if you want."

"No problem at all, Steve. I can sweep it up. I've heard this is funny," she said politely.

"He's the best!" I almost yelled back at her. The other two people in the store turned toward me, and I could feel their eyes on me and my dirt trail. I felt more guilty about the mess, and I wondered what those other two customers thought of me. I'm sure they were judging me, but in that moment, I couldn't take time to explain myself to them.

I had waited three months, and I could barely wait a second longer to get home. I felt such relief to finally have my hands on "'Weird Al' in 3-D." "Weird Al" Yankovic was a comedic genius and probably the coolest person I had ever heard of, maybe even more than Uncle Steve, Uncle Donn, or Ray Christensen. *Oh, do I hope they included the words with the cassette tape. I love when they do that.*

It took forever to ride my bike back home, and I saw that old, gold Chrysler Cordoba in our driveway. Mom was home. "Hi, Mom. I got it!" I ran to my room. I used my teeth to get that annoying plastic off and fold open the case and, yes, lyrics were included! I fumbled to get the cassette the right way into the stereo and hit play.

The first thing I heard were the distinctive notes from the synthesizer of Michael Jackson's "Beat It," but this was better than that; this was "Eat It." It was a bit hard to sing along through my massive smile and laughter. *I wonder what Michael Jackson thinks of this parody.* I imagined him laughing just like me. The music kept getting better with a parody of "The Safety Dance" called "The Brady Bunch," and so many more—eleven amazing songs I had been waiting for forever!

I was exhausted but so happy after the day's events and listening through the entire cassette. I was completely in my own world. Mom hadn't told me dinner was ready, but I figured she was giving me space, knowing how important this day was to me. I was sitting on my floor with my back leaned against the side of my bed, my arms still caked with dirt, sweat, and gopher germs. I realized I forgot to take off my shoes. There must've been dirt all over the carpet on the steps and in the hallway.

Now I knew mom must be giving me my space because that was worthy of her yelling at me. My dusty fingers rested on the rewind and play buttons, ready to listen again to the best parts. I was going to memorize these and be the funniest person in the school. People were going to think I was the greatest. If they had any doubts before, they wouldn't now. I was going to be the most liked person at school, maybe in the county!

I wondered how talented people were discovered. I suppose that never happened in rural Minnesota, but if anyone was going to be discovered, it would be me. I didn't even have my driver's license and had already written more than fifty full-length parodies. Each one had been neatly typed on my mom's basement typewriter and organized alphabetically in a leftover school folder.

I was so funny. Every time I sang them, or even read them, I laughed until I was almost crying. I didn't like to brag, but I felt like I was very clever, and someday the people in my school would realize that and tell me how awesome I was, or at least no one would dare pick on me. They would regret not being my friend when they saw how far this parody-writing took me; when people were coming from miles around to see this quirky kid make them laugh.

And when that happened, I would know I must be okay because that many people couldn't all be wrong.

CHAPTER 3:

LIFE AFTER LOSING MY LUNCH AND MY LIGAMENTS

Like I expected, freshman year of high school was intimidating. I hated riding the bus, and bullies stalked the hallways. I was grateful for the friends I had, and it seemed like a few new kids had some things in common with me. I learned to use humor to get the right people to notice me and to amuse those I was afraid of. I still dabbled in jingle-singing and parody-writing at home, but jokes had become my primary go-to strategy for making people laugh and finding acceptance. I regretted some of my jokes, but I was desperate for people to accept me, and laughter was the best medicine I knew.

Whenever I heard a group of people laughing in the hallways, I assumed they were laughing at me. Sometimes it was obvious because they were looking at me, but even when they weren't looking my way, I couldn't help but think it was somehow about me. Considering how much laughter happened in the school every day, this was a tough way to live. I pretended they were laughing at one of my jokes or maybe even heard one of my amazing parodies, even though I would never risk sharing with most of them. In situations like that, it helped to have a great imagination.

Although I didn't have the confidence to stand in front of people and sing, even as part of a choir, I had found a good outlet for my love of music through the high school band. I was initially reluctant to join band because every school concert I had been to for my brother was terrible. It was so boring, and he was always practicing at home. But Mom thought I should, and I heard band was an easy credit. And since several members of the Fredlunds had musical skills, I was sure my new family would think it was great.

I'd picked out my instrument a few years earlier during the fifth-grade band open house. I struggled figuring out what instrument to play. Drums seemed awesome, but they were very expensive and too loud for our house. My buddy had an idea. "You should play trombone with me. You love *Music Man!*" He started pretending he was marching as he hummed "Seventy-six trombones," and I started laughing. Neither of us knew he would one day regret talking me into this.

Throughout middle school, I thought about quitting band. I never practiced, and I wasn't very good, not realizing how those two things might be related. I brought my trombone home every day because our grades were docked if we didn't. Bringing it on the bus was a pain but worth it for the better grade, and good grades were extremely important.

Band turned out to be a good thing as I started my first year of high school. It was a good fit for me socially and helped me feel like part of a community. I already knew many of the kids, which helped. Our neighboring town had their own middle school, but the kids came to high school with us. I met a few of these new kids through band, and they seemed to think I was all right, and I thought the same thing about them. Some of them were even into hacky-sack and Dungeons & Dragons. I did love music, and even though a lot of band music was boring, it was cool how we could each do our own individual thing and combine it into something better.

I felt safe in band, and in many ways, it was the hour every day when I didn't have to sit through boring lectures, listen to people smack their gum, or watch football players try to impress cheerleaders. Band was my oasis away from the annoying chaos of most high school classrooms.

And then, just like that, everything changed. We were practicing one of the pieces for our upcoming concert, and I started feeling a bit queasy. My mouth was watering, which happened right before I threw up. I didn't want to get up and draw attention to myself, but my stomach was not having it. *Oh, please don't throw up,* I thought. I could tell I was turning red and starting to sweat, but then it subsided for a moment, and I thought I would be fine. Back and forth it went, but I thought I could keep it at bay until class was over. *I've got this.*

Then it happened. My high G in fourth position was joined in an ominous duet by what sounded like the bark of a sea lion. *No, no, no. This cannot be happening.* It could, and it did, and it was violent. Vomit came out with force and volume. I was literally throwing up into my trombone. Some of the chunks were forced through the mouthpiece and into the brass slide, while the rest ricocheted back. The funneled mouthpiece acted like a deflection shield directing massive quantities at other trombonists and even beyond.

It didn't stop there when as another wave hit. This one had less chunks and more liquid. The good news was that more of it fit through the mouthpiece and into the slide, but the bad news was the distance the rest of it traveled. Splatter was all over my glasses and dripped from my cheeks. I didn't know if I should lick my lips, wipe them with my hand, or just start spitting like someone who had a gnat fly into their mouth. The smell was awful and the moment crippling.

Amid the chaos, I immediately recognized the bigger picture of this situation, the impact this would have on my already tenuous social standing. All my effort to hide my childish passions for parodies and statistics had now gone to waste. What was the point of trying to act normal and fit in if I was going to throw it away by blowing chunks in the band room?

Not everyone had noticed yet, so I slowly set my trombone down. "I'm sorry. I'm sorry." I forced words through the strings of vomit strewn between my teeth. *Should I spit or swallow or just let it sit my mouth?*

I stepped back behind my chair, covering my mouth and hoping no one realized I was now drooling vomit into my hand, praying a third round could be held back. Little by little the music was stopping, and I felt eyes on me as I walked quickly to the side door, which thankfully led directly outside the school.

In that moment, I decided I was never going to be in band again, and I may have to tell Mom I now needed to be homeschooled. Mercifully, the third and fourth rounds waited until I was outside. My left hand held me against the rough brown and red brick of the school while my right-hand foraged for grass to wipe my hands and face.

A welcomed diversion and smile found my still vomit-laden lips as I remembered the "better get a bucket" scene from the movie *Monty Python's The Meaning of Life*. I spent the next twenty minutes cleaning myself, planning how I would quit band, and wondering what it smelled like back in the band room. Other than a couple of parents walking to their cars, I was alone. I wanted to be invisible, so this was perfect. I wanted to burrow underground like a gopher, but not like one in Tom and Ellie's yard.

Finally the bell rang, and I cracked open the door to make sure everyone was gone. I snuck back in, and my teacher had started cleaning my trombone. I was grateful but mortified. Without words, I took over for him, rinsing it and starting to pack it up, doing all I could to not let the smell make me hurl again. A nervous chuckle escaped as I cleaned and put the mouthpiece deflection shield into the case.

This moment was defining. This would be how people remembered me for the rest of my high school life. I was the "kid who puked in band." This would be a story my teacher would share with other teachers, which would become the story told as they gathered with their families and friends. I could hear it: "You are never going to believe what happened in this guy's band class."

I enjoyed this teacher, and I thought he liked me too, but he certainly wouldn't think I was okay after this, and I didn't have enough confidence to lose his approval. I needed to try to save this moment, but I struggled with the right words to say. I fell back on my humor. "Do you think that last note was a little flat?"

He smiled, and I smiled. He would never forget what I did in his classroom, but maybe if he thought I was funny, he would still think I was an okay person. This would have to do because I was literally never going to go to band again. And I didn't—literally, never. I dropped band the next day.

I had already given up on most of my public jingle-singing and parody-writing, saving it for when I was completely alone. Band had become the only public outlet for my music and creativity, and now, it was gone. I lamented how at least I had my humor and passion for football.

As great as I was at keeping football stats and remembering team fight songs, I was equally bad as an athlete. Luckily, our community was small enough that there were no sports tryouts, so anyone who wanted could play on the school teams. I played football, basketball, and baseball, and I loved saying that at family gatherings. Grandpa Fredlund was a star athlete at the same high school, so it was a good connection point with my family.

I was only put into games during "garbage time," when the score was so lopsided the outcome was decided before the game was officially over. The coaches put players like me in, probably to make our parents happy but mostly to make sure the good athletes didn't get hurt when there was nothing to play for. I really liked the practices and camaraderie, and on game day we all got something on our locker, even us reserve players. It felt great to be on a team because I felt part of something bigger and more important than myself. I would stay part of the team as long as showers weren't required after practice, like they were after gym.

But just like how band went away, I was about to also lose high school sports.

All things considered, freshman year wasn't so bad although I was glad it was summer. I effectively counterbalanced the trombone vomit with playing sports and being funny. I had a few good friends, and I thought most of the other kids thought I was okay or at least didn't pick on me as much as they picked on some other kids. My teachers loved that I worked hard and asked questions.

We had a massive yard, and although we had a riding lawnmower, my job was to use the push mower to get the trickier parts. I filled it with gas, checked the oil, pushed the bubble a couple of times to prime it, and then started pulling the rope. Normally it started on the second pull, but on this day it had a bit of an attitude—four, five, six pulls.

"Come on, you dumb thing." Frustrated, I kicked the plastic tires. I gave it one final pull with everything I had. I heard a ripping noise coming from my left knee as I crumpled to the ground and saw stars. The pain was indescribable, leaving me screaming like I had never screamed before. I could open my eyes just barely enough to see what was happening. I saw my kneecap on the side of my leg, which was causing everything below the knee to stick out at an angle. I had dislocated my knee before, but never anything like this.

No one was home to hear my screaming, and if I didn't do something soon, I feared I would black out from the pain. I knew what needed to be done to get it back into place, or at least I knew what worked before when it just slightly dislocated, but I didn't know if I had the courage to fight through the pain to do what must be done. I had to try because what other choice did I have?

I dug my heel into the driveway, which shot pain throughout my entire body, and then used my hands to push myself backward across the gravel. *Pop!* The kneecap flipped back over the edge of the joint and slid back into the groove where it was supposed to be as my lower leg realigned. My screaming stopped, but the pain was still very real, and my mind raced to try and figure out what that ripping noise was.

The next day, I was in an operating room getting two torn ligaments repaired. I spent the entire summer on crutches. I was so discouraged. I had already given up parody-writing and jingle-singing and just quit band, the only musical outlet I had left. I had already given up keeping stats and being so passionate about college football, and now I had to give up playing sports. I was really struggling, and I had no idea how I was going to fit in.

Every good Lutheran church in the mid-1980s had a youth group leader who was young, relevant, and looked like he was just pulled from the set of *Starsky and Hutch*. The youth leader at my church was named Keith, and man, was he cool!

"Steve, think about what you are good at," he told me one night at youth group as I tried to beat him in foosball, even with my crutches. "Sometimes when God shuts a door, he opens a window." *Wait, what? God shut these doors and took these things I love from me? Or do you mean God is literally shutting doors and opening windows, which is sort of creepy?* "What I mean is, maybe this gives you a chance to spend more time on things like school and some of your other activities."

I liked Keith, and I thought he was someone I should listen to. Other than the window and door thing, he made a lot of sense, so I would follow his plan to focus on what I was good at and not waste time dwelling on things I lost. It was time I started thinking about my future, which was realistically never going to be something as outlandish as a professional athlete, trombonist, play-by-play guy, sports agent, jingle-singer, or parody-writer. In three short years I would be graduating high school and becoming an adult. Keith thought it was time to grow up and become more practical, and I thought he was right. My future happiness would have to come from good grades that led to good jobs that led to good money.

I was off the crutches as I started my sophomore year with a new focus on smart-kid activities. For the next few years, I stockpiled accolades, success, and the approval of my teachers and family with my prowess in Math League, Knowledge Bowl, Mock Trial, and Business Professionals of America. I engaged my humor and creative sides when needed, but they were fully secondary now to my intelligence. The source of my validation shifted from "You are so funny" to more adult-centered comments like "You are so smart." This made sense to me because being funny and clever felt like little kid things while being smart and responsible was how adults succeed. As a result, trading the door for a window launched me on a path toward being a successful adult, which was the right kind of adult to be.

Throughout high school, I did a good job of keeping my creative use of humor in check, recognizing it was not as acceptable to many of the adults whose approval I now relied on to feel like I was doing things right. But sometimes, in moments of weakness, I let my guard down and reverted to what made me feel accepted when I was younger.

As I neared the end of my senior year, I was preparing to go to Louisville, Kentucky. A few of us, including my buddy Jeff, qualified for the national competition with Business Professionals of America. I would be competing with the nation's best in accounting and business math.

We had a fundraiser to help cover the cost of the trip, and I had been asked to do an announcement over the school loudspeaker to promote it. The script was great, perfect for the radio voice I had practiced, which was my unique blend of Ray Christensen and Uncle Donn. After a deep breath, I pushed the button and shared my message with the world, or at least the high school.

It was going great! The women working in the office had huge smiles on their faces as I smoothly flowed over words like an Olympic hurdle champion. I reached the crescendo at the end, and it was perfect. But then I had my moment of weakness where I fell back into childish Steve. In my failure, an unplanned ending slipped out. "And when you go there, tell 'em Lila sent ya!"

Lila was our faculty advisor, but first names were not allowed when talking about faculty members. I started to worry a bit about what I said as I returned to my accounting class. When I entered the room, my classmates clapped and gave me high-fives, and the teacher smiled at me. In this moment, I remembered how good it felt to be accepted for being creative and funny.

This feeling ended abruptly with a knock on the door. I saw a familiar face pressed up against the narrow rectangle window. It was Mrs. Renstrom, who I referred to as Lila. She saw me and did not look pleased. She didn't wait for an answer but opened the door and gestured for me to join her in the hallway. I lowered my head and walked sheepishly toward the door through a subtle chorus of "Oooh, you're in trouble!"

I received a mild scolding about using proper names and being respectful. Frankly, I deserved worse. I thought she was slightly amused but couldn't admit it because it would take away from the lesson. As I returned to the class, I received a few more high-fives and smiles. I appreciated their support, but I was reminded how I needed to focus on being smart and responsible more than being funny if I wanted people of influence in this world to take me seriously and validate me.

Throughout high school I had a few more lapses in judgment like that, where my former habits of using creative humor to neutralize disharmony or gain validation showed themselves. But in each situation, I was reminded my long-term happiness was going to be found in valuing my education and applying my intellect. I loved making people laugh, but the older I got, the more I realized those around me were far more interested in what I knew and what I could produce than whether I could make them laugh.

It took me my whole high school career to really understand that, but finally it all seemed to make sense, and just in time to decide about where to go to college. It was good I was not going into that decision still focused on how much I enjoyed big school college football or how I liked to use creative humor to make people laugh.

CHAPTER 4:

YOU JUST HAVE TO ASK
THE RIGHT PEOPLE

Focusing on studying throughout high school paid off, and with the financial aid I expected, I was able to go to just about any college I wanted. I enjoyed applying to different schools; some of them just to see if they would accept me, like Harvard. It was such a great feeling every time an envelope came in the mail starting with "Congratulations future class of 1992!" I knew they were form letters, but I saved them, pulling them out every time I needed to feel valued and wanted.

I used one of my old football stat notebooks to create a list of colleges that accepted me and whether they offered any scholarship money. I made a few other notes about cost, enrollment, and location. The notebook reminded me of younger days keeping stats from the radio or for Uncle Donn, which then also reminded me of those great times on the farm watching college football with Uncle Steve. A huge smile came to my face, and I gave myself permission to remember how happy I was during those times.

I struggled to know what would make me that happy in my future. I hadn't been taught, but what I had caught was that happiness for an adult started with going to the right college and then getting the right job at the right company. So, I'd start there. What was the right college for me?

Many of the schools on my list were big ones, directly out of my memories from the farm: Ohio State, Michigan, USC, and Notre Dame. Another big school called Texas Christian University, or TCU, had offered me a full-ride scholarship. They were in Fort Worth, Texas, which was close to Dallas where Uncle Steve had moved.

As I started to analyze the options, I felt naïve to what factors I should really consider. I basically ignored the big universities on my list, not because they didn't sound awesome but because I knew my attraction to them was purely emotional, not rational. Instead, I focused on the names of smaller schools closer to home like Augsburg, Hamline, and St. Cloud State. But I didn't know how to make this decision. Making the wrong choice could have a negative impact on my life while the right one could catapult me to success and certainly impress my family and friends.

I was truly missing the feeling of empowerment to make the best decision for me and what I wanted, but I wouldn't realize that until a few decades later. All I needed was a small nudge from a trusted adult to go to a big school. If somebody had only asked me, "What have you always dreamed college would be?" …but that question was never asked. I continued secretly holding on to the big school temptation, which increased as I learned about their extracurriculars like a cappella singing groups and comedy clubs.

The temptation subsided a bit once I had a girlfriend because I didn't want to be as far away as Texas or California, or even Michigan or Indiana. Naturally, I was torn, and my mind seemed to torment me. *It's only for four years, and it would be so much fun to try something way outside of what I know as safe.* The decision was stressing me out, but I needed to make it so I could move on. I needed to find an expert who could tell me the right next step.

That expert was right under my nose the entire time. I finally found out what the school guidance counselor did and set up an appointment for advice on this now-heavy decision. I was nervous but hopeful about the conversation.

On my way to the appointment, I took several turns as I weaved down the hallway looking for the office. I made a mental note of the pattern of left and right turns, knowing I could just reverse the order to get back out. Just in case he could see me in the hallway, I made sure to not walk too fast so I appeared too eager or too slow so I appeared scared or disinterested. I was wearing my purple sweater I wore for senior pictures, the one my friend's mom thought I looked good in.

I knocked and was quickly greeted. "Come in." I was relieved he was in his office, because that meant there was no way he could have seen me walking down the hallway moments before. I immediately realized I was in the right place. Printed certificates on the wall, thick books on nice wooden shelves, pictures of successful-looking people in frames on the desk, and two open chairs that looked like they might be leather were there. As I looked around, I was interrupted by the young but smart-looking counselor who had come out from behind his desk with his hand extended.

"Hello, Steve. It's nice to meet you. Please have a seat."

I carefully started moving toward the chairs. "Thank you. It's nice to be. I mean, meeting... it's nice to meet you also." I sounded like I'd never walked and talked at the same time. I knew how to make a first impression. I sat down and... yeah, it was leather.

"I understand you want to talk about college."

I took a deep breath. "Yes. Thank you for seeing me. I am not sure who to talk to. I want to go to college, but I don't know where. Is that something you can help me figure out?"

"It's my specialty," he said with a wry smile. *Is he joking? Is it really his specialty? Or does he not know anything about it and is covering it up with humor? I know that game.* My furrowed brow gave him the clue he needed to move from humor to seriousness. "I can definitely help you with that, Steve."

He then spoke with authority, like it really was his specialty. His confidence created trust, and I hung on every word he said. "I've been looking at your file, and it looks like you are super smart, especially in math. Would you say you tend to be more introverted?"

I was distracted by this file bombshell he just dropped. *I didn't know I had a file. What's in this file? Does it have information about vomiting in band or when I got detention?* He reminded me we were having a conversation by repeating the question, "Steve, would you say you tend to be more introverted?"

"Yes. But this year…"

He interrupted me before I could explain how I'd been coming out of my shell, that I was in the school musical and had a great time at the all-night party and the senior class trip, or that I had my first serious girlfriend who had given me so much confidence. I hated being interrupted. It made me feel unimportant. But if he didn't need those details, I guess they didn't matter. I didn't bother breaking in to make sure he had the full story. It was so easy for me to assume other people had the right answers.

"Do you live in town or out in the country? "

"In the country." I was so curious where he was going with this.

"Well, Steve, I would say your best bet is a small campus here in Minnesota where they have a good math program." He wrote down the names of four local colleges and handed it over to me. "Do you think you can make one of these work for you?"

Is that really it? All he needs to know to tell me where to go to college is that I'm smart, introverted, and live in the country? Shouldn't he know about my passion for college football and that I did stats with my uncle and that I love to make people laugh and that I've written so many parodies like my hero "Weird Al" and that I've recently become passionate about playing tennis? I knew he was the expert, but I felt underwhelmed and disappointed.

But the school trusted him to hand out college advice, so I assumed he knew what he was talking about, even with such limited information. *Maybe some of that other stuff is in my file?* My instinct was saying to trust myself, but I didn't listen. I overrode myself, trusting the authority instead.

I forgot I was still in his office when he interrupted my spiraling. "Steve?" I shook myself back into the moment and made eye contact again. He stood and reached out his hand. Like a Pavlovian dog, I reacted to him without even thinking. I followed his lead, stood up, and shook his hand. "I wish you all the best, Steve. I know you will do great things and make the Bluejackets proud!"

"Thank you, sir. I will." I was confused, and my brow was furrowed, but I made my way to the door he politely held open for me.

By the time I was back in the main office, reversing my way out of the labyrinth, my hesitancy had faded. I convinced myself he was an expert and therefore right about the small local school being what was best for me. *If nothing else, I now have a plan. I should have had this meeting earlier. I wasted so much time trying to figure it out on my own.*

Cross-referencing the counselor's list with mine quickly narrowed it down to two choices, and within a week I was on a walking tour of Augsburg College in Minneapolis. Four of us, all high schoolers, were led around the small campus by a peppy-upbeat sophomore music major.

I was more comfortable asking questions of her than the counselor, maybe because I considered her more like a peer even though she clearly was an expert about the college. She answered my inquiries about the food plan, underground tunnels, gym hours, and how to get across the river to the University of Minnesota, just in case I wanted to go to a Big Ten football game.

We were almost back to Old Main where the tour started when she asked, "Does anyone have any final questions?"

I wanted to know how she compared Augsburg to other schools. "Yeah. So, based on your experience so far, why do you think we should come here instead of somewhere else?"

"Oh my gosh—just everything! It's, like, totally amazing. You all have to come here!" Internally, I was rolling my eyes and maybe even wincing a bit at her lack of a compelling, logical argument. But her energy was infectious, and she made me feel like she would personally like to have me there. Maybe it would be a good fit for me. I understood why they had her doing this job.

I thought I had made my decision, but I needed one more person's approval: Keith, the youth leader. I found him the next day at church and asked if he had a minute to talk. "Sure. What's up?" Keith always made me feel so cool just by talking with him.

"I'm making my college decision, and I want to know what you think."

"Well, college is a very personal choice. Think about what you love to do, what you want to learn, and what kind of experiences you want to have." He brought up the very things I had been trying to push down and not be tempted by. *Maybe I should have talked with Keith before I went on the school tour. Ugh, I can't reopen this whole decision.* Augsburg seemed like it would be fine, and I just needed him to say it was fine also.

"I have thought a lot about it, and I think I have made my choice, and I am just wondering what you think of that choice." He signaled for me to share. "I think I'm going to Augsburg. Do you think that's okay?"

"Whoa, I didn't see that coming. I figured you to be a big-time university kind of guy. But Augsburg is cool. I have a lot of friends who went there. Did you know it's a Lutheran school? We might be able to find a bit of scholarship money for you. Did you know Bill is planning on going there too?"

"Yeah, I heard about Bill," I said even though I didn't know him very well. "So, you think it's an okay choice?"

"It's a good school, but it doesn't matter what I think. Do you think it's the right choice?"

My brain quickly processed all the information that had led me to thinking this was the right choice. I never had reason to cross it off my original list made in my old stats notebook. It was only an hour from my home and girlfriend. The counselor had it on his list of four. The student tour guide thought it was awesome and personally told me I should go there. They had intramural tennis. Keith had friends who went there and thought the church could give me a scholarship.

"Yes. Yes, I think it's the right choice." There, it's settled—finally.

That summer was filled with work and getting ready to leave home for the first time. I didn't really know what to expect, but I was excited for the adventure.

Starting college felt like a fresh start, which was both good and bad. I didn't know anyone on campus, and making new friendships was not something I was very good at. But I also hadn't been labeled, and no one knew about my childish jingle-singing or parody-writing, and certainly no one knew about the great trombone vomit incident of 1984.

All around me it felt like students were on a mission to explore life, learn about new ways of seeing the world, challenge the beliefs they inherited, and pursue their true authentic selves. It seemed most of them chose a liberal arts school to get to the truth of who they truly were. This message was reinforced during orientation as well as the required course designed to help with our transition to college.

I wasn't doing any of that. I was just trying to fit in and do things right. I just wanted my classmates and professors to like, accept, and validate me. I just wanted to feel like I was okay.

In those first few days of college, all I knew about fitting in was that I should study hard and maintain a great GPA. The professors made it very clear through their semester syllabus and grading rubric this was going to be a lot tougher than high school. My road to future happiness, which would be found in great jobs at great companies, started right now, with working hard in class to maintain the GPA that would get me recognition when I graduated. So far at this point, I found this was the only thing that would get me the validation I was looking for. I trusted others would emerge as I went forward.

"Steve! Steve!" I heard a vaguely familiar female voice calling my name in the dining hall. I wasn't sure she was looking for me until she started moving in my direction and made eye contact. "It's me, Natalie. I was your tour guide in the spring."

"Oh, wow. Yeah, I thought you looked familiar." I stood up and shook her hand. I was sitting with some new friends who I'd started playing basketball with between classes. I could hear them start to chuckle, thinking it was hilarious I shook her hand.

"I'm so glad you chose Augsburg. Everyone in your tour group also decided to come here!" She moved her focus from me to the entire table. "Hey, my house is having a party on Friday if any of you want to come."

Jim chimed in. He was by far the coolest of all of us at that table. "Yeah, great. See ya there." We nodded, maybe a little too aggressively, as Natalie waved goodbye and moved her way across the room. It felt like it was starting to happen.

Little by little, I was connecting with those people who would help me have the right college experience.

In my first three years of college, I became friends with a lot of people who helped me have fun. This started with Natalie's party but continued with many late-night pizzas and card games, sometimes playing five hundred until our morning classes started. I performed in the musical *Godspell*, won the annual lip sync contest every year, and was even crowned Mr. Urness, which was a competition in our freshman dorm that included a talent show, swimsuit appearance, and answering an "ultimate question."

Some of these experiences leveraged the creativity of my youth, even performing in front of people, and it felt good. They were foolish pursuits and probably not lined up with what I should be more focused on, but I was encouraged to do them by my new friends. They created a lot of laughs and fun memories, but I knew they were just the peripheral things to enjoy amid the backdrop of my more serious life that was emerging.

By now I had completely forgotten about my passion for college football. Augsburg was a lower-division school that couldn't even get fifteen hundred people in the stands for homecoming. During my time in college, the team's combined record was five wins and thirty-four losses—not exactly something to get fired up about. As a matter of fact, I stopped watching college football altogether.

Most of my time in college was spent working and studying. Despite a helpful financial aid package, I had to take out significant loans and work to cover the rest. With each year I increased how much I worked, and by my junior year I was working more than thirty hours every week.

My plan was to double major in math and English because I loved creative writing. In fact, the seniors majoring in theater performed one of my screenplays, *Hank and Frank*. But my hatred of British literature turned that major to a minor.

I still had no idea how I was going to use a math degree after graduation when my college advisor asked if I knew what an actuary was. I had never even heard of it. "It's ranked the number one job in America, and I think you would be great at it." He explained more about the job, really focusing on the long, brutal process of passing a series of difficult exams, and the first one was happening soon if I wanted to give it a shot.

"That sounds interesting. I will give it a shot." It was really that simple. One conversation, no personal research, and no true understanding of the daunting nature of the exams required for an actuarial career. I totally trusted my advisor, and if he thought this was the right thing to do, let's do it. Whenever I saw him, he called me, "Mr. Actuary."

But there's one thing I didn't tell my advisor or anyone else in my life. It had been a secret throughout high school and college. I didn't actually love math, at least not like my college classmates. Yes, I was a well-decorated mathlete, and even the college math courses were easy other than abstract algebra, which I thought was pointless. But I didn't love math.

The trouble was, I had no idea what I would even do if it wasn't math, so why not just do what I was good at? Who truly loves their job anyway? My math aptitude was a gift, and who was I to squander it? Nothing else had validated me with the influential people in my life more than being good at math. So, bring on the actuarial exams, and let's really show people what I was capable of.

CHAPTER 5:

A WEDDING, A SALAMANDER, AND A PILE OF SNAKES

———

I leaned over toward the pastor and asked, "Do normal people sweat like this?" I was trying to deflect the stress of the situation as I stood in front of this church with three hundred people staring at me.

I felt so exposed, standing there in my rented tuxedo and fancy shoes, waiting to meet Tracy at the altar. I scanned every pew, making eye contact with so many friends and family, some I hadn't seen for years. *When is the music finally going to start?* I softened as every face made me feel loved and accepted; so many reminders of times spent together and their encouraging words over the years. This was true on both sides of the church, as Tracy's family had come to mean so much to me those past three years of dating—from her Smith family reunions to playing the card game May I with the Hollands. It became a futile effort to hold back the tears.

Maybe they are just here to support Tracy. I guess it doesn't matter who she marries. They would be here. I think they like me, but maybe they are just here because they love Tracy and must show their support. Maybe they think she is making a mistake getting married this young or marrying me. Stress has a powerful way of eroding my confidence.

I hyped myself back up by thinking how far ahead I was compared to most twenty-one-year-olds. With still a year left in college, I had a good-paying part-time job at 3M, and I already knew what career I wanted. I had come a long way from being quirky little Stevie Rice from Dalbo. I was a grown man who was making it and had a world of potential. *There, that's better. I know I'm worthy of this woman and her family.*

The processional music finally started, cueing the ushers to escort our immediate families to their reserved seats. The music and their walking were painfully slow. *Seriously, guys,* I thought. *Let's go.*

As Tracy's mom came down the aisle, I thought of how much food she gave us every time we came home from college, and how their dog bit me the first time I went to their house.

Next came my mom. She looked so great and very happy. I prayed I made her proud; that I was becoming who she hoped I would. She had been through so much, worked so hard, and always made us a priority. I was not so sure I always deserved it, but I really had been so loved. I gave up even trying to hold back the tears or wiping them from my face. The dam had burst, and there was nothing to be done.

The last time I tried that hard to hold something inside, I was trying to keep from vomiting into my trombone. I glanced over at a couple of friends who were in the band room that fateful day, and I wondered if they were thinking the same thing as we exchanged smiles. I was surprised they stayed my friends after my epic collapse that day, or maybe they became my friends later and weren't aware of it. That made more sense. *Why can't I shut off my brain, even for my wedding?* I just wanted to be in the moment, yet my thoughts continued their annoying background hum.

One by one the groomsmen came forward, each escorting a bridesmaid. Each of them meant so much to me, and right then I wanted to give each a huge hug and thanks for being so nice to me and tell them how much they meant to me. But I also wanted to completely ignore them, hoping that would keep me from completely embarrassing myself with emotional outbursts. The pastor was now too far away to ask what I should do, so I defaulted to what a good adult would do. They each got a firm handshake, a smile, and an awe-shucks shrug.

The processional music shifted, and everyone stood as Tracy entered the back of the church with her dad. She always looked good, but that day she was stunning. A wave of fear hit when it dawned on me that in less than an hour, I was going to be a husband. I was going to be married with a ring on my finger. I was excited to marry and prove I had arrived as an adult, but what did it mean to be a husband? *This isn't a mistake. Is it?* As she got closer, I could see her face more clearly. The way she looked at me melted every concern. She had a knack for grounding me when I started spiraling with worry and questions.

"Who gives this woman to be married?" *I am so lucky. This is perfect. I love her so much. I'm glad I'm getting married. I will be a great husband. I've got this.*

The wedding was beautiful although I barely listened to anything anyone said. I felt the love and acceptance of Tracy and everyone in the church. People we loved were readers, singers, greeters, groomsmen, and bridesmaids, and so many others were there supporting us as we kicked off our married life.

At the reception so many of my high school and college buddies stuck around, reminiscing about the old times and taking a group picture that I knew I would cherish forever. Over the years I had nagging thoughts if some of them even liked me or if they were just being nice to me in school. On that day, those questions were answered.

My brother, Larry, was scrambling to make the day fun and memorable, with little surprises like bringing me a bottle of pop in the reception line and decorating the car. I felt a bit guilty because I was not nearly this good to him when he got married about three weeks before, but it really made me feel great to have him take care of his little brother like that.

Those rented fancy shoes were doing a number on my feet, knees, and back, but it helped to have ZZ Top's "Sharp Dressed Man" lyrics running through my head all day. Memories of performing a lip sync to that song made me smile through the discomfort.

Our time came to leave, and so many people stuck around to wish us the best. I couldn't believe they were still there on that beautiful late summer Saturday, especially since the college football season kicked off. I felt honored they chose to spend their precious time with us.

Larry pulled our car into the church turnaround for our exit. He had done a great job of decorating it, but it was still a crappy old Chevy Malibu with no hubcaps and windows that didn't roll down. *Seriously, how could I not think of upgrading for today? Why didn't I rent a car or at least borrow someone else's?* I calmed down as I read the fun messages written all over and the old shoes he tied to the back bumper.

We were moments away from the grand finale of our wedding when we would leave the church to the cheers of our family and friends. The moment had arrived when we could finally get off our feet and talk about the big day, just the two of us. Apparently, our family put a fully loaded cooler in our car so we would have some food, drink, and snacks for the drive down to our apartment. Everyone was so sweet and supportive. I didn't eat much at the reception, so I was starving and excited to see what they put in the cooler.

"You got a flat!" someone yelled. Word quickly made it up the stairs to us as we were just about to take that first step through our adoring fans. I'm not sure why I found this moment so funny, but it struck me as hilarious. And while I was excited to get off my feet, open the cooler, and talk about the day with Tracy, this would provide a few more moments feeling fully saturated in the love of our family and friends. I needed to soak up this validation. It was healing for my past and would be needed for my future.

Like a superhero, Dave, one of my mom's friends, immediately sprang into action. He handed someone his suit coat, rolled up his sleeves, pulled the jack and spare from the trunk, grabbed the lug wrench, and started loosening the nuts. Maybe it was good we didn't have any hubcaps on the car after all. This dude was still in his suit, kneeling on the cement, selflessly serving us on our big day. *I bet Dave is always the first person to jump into a situation where there is a need. People must love this guy.* I recognized I wanted to be like him, the first to jump in when there was a need. He was doing more than changing a tire. He was giving me clarity on what it meant to be a friend, husband, and hopefully someday a dad.

I had never felt more validated than on our wedding day—from Tracy and my brother to our families and all our friends who were there. On that day, I knew I was loved and accepted. I knew I was okay, and I wanted to hold on to that feeling forever.

Some people always know they are okay; that no matter what they see or hear, they have the self-confidence to never question themselves. I don't have that. I need others to validate me. I am pretty sure most people generally think I'm okay, but I need them to say it, or to do something that reassures me it is true. That's why I knew the feeling on our wedding day would be fleeting. I would need to prove myself to others over and over, not for their sake but for mine, to not lose that feeling that I really was okay.

Tracy made it easy. She was easily impressed and grateful for the simple things I did, like making sure all our bank accounts, bills, and student loans were set up as joint accounts. I made sure her driver's license and everything else successfully made the change from Anderson to Fredlund.

She appreciated being married to someone so responsible, and she let me know.

I also knew Tracy's parents loved and accepted me, but I couldn't rest on my laurels. I needed to keep doing things they were grateful for so they would have no choice but to keep validating me as their son-in-law. So, impressing and serving them was important to me, even if it meant overcoming my own fears to prove myself worthy.

Ever since we started dating, Tracy had never let me even look in her parents' basement, much less go down there. I didn't really understand why. It was no big deal, just an unfinished, cement block basement of an old farmhouse. Not being able to go down there made my mind run wild. *Is it possible I married into a family of serial killers who keep bodies in basement freezers? Is there a torture room or a bloody table saw? Maybe I watch too much crime television.* Maybe, but the visceral reaction Tracy had about me looking in the basement led me to believe it must be something like that. Nothing else made sense.

This was why I was so confused when she told me I needed to go to her parents' house and into the basement. "I'm not allowed to even look down there. Why do you need me to go down there now?"

"There's a salamander, and my mom is afraid to go downstairs," Tracy explained.

"Oh, now I see how it is! I've begged for years just to look in the basement, even wondering if you are serial killers, but noooo, I'm not allowed. But now that there's a salamander, no one has a problem with it." When we arrived at her parents' house and they reiterated their request, my response to them had less sarcasm. "No problem. Happy to help."

Confession time: I think salamanders are gross, and I do not want to go near them, much less touch them. But what choice did I have? Did I say they are gross, and I didn't want to, showing myself as weak and risking their acceptance? I needed to prove I was a worthy son-in-law. I made sure the basement door closed behind me. I didn't want them seeing how scared I was or hearing me yelp if the four-inch slimy lizard moved toward me in attack mode.

Having captured the beast, I came back upstairs bursting through the door in victory. As the conquering hero, I took the critter outside where it belonged. Tracy gave me her "Way to go, babe" smile, her mom gave me a hug, and her dad gave me a pat on the back. *That's right. It's good y'all have me around.*

The next spring, Tracy's dad told me about a barn where he stored hay. A bunch of bales were left in there, but now mice had chewed through the twine, leaving loose hay everywhere. He wanted to store more hay in there, but first he must get all the loose stuff cleaned up. I seized the opportunity.

"If it would be helpful, I can take care of that." I had a lot to prove to this long-time farmer to make sure he knew I had the work ethic required to be a good husband and son-in-law. He might have only seen me as a math nerd, but I also wanted him to see me as an asset to him, his daughter, and the entire family.

While I couldn't match the strength of his handshake, I could make up for it by taking on tough projects he didn't have time for. He accepted my offer and dropped me off at the barn with leather gloves and a couple of pitchforks. After explaining what he wanted done, he left me to it.

The hay was literally infested with snakes. Apparently, where there were mice chewing through twine, there were snakes looking for an easy meal. I was thankful the pitchfork had four tines to increase my chances at stabbing them. After every scoop of my pitchfork, I stood back for a moment to see if snakes came slithering out. I started the project deathly afraid of snakes, but over the course of four hours, I started getting over my fear. It's amazing the confidence that comes from having a sharp weapon, work boots, and thick leather gloves, along with the driving force of knowing the validation I would receive when the job was finished.

I passed the time mentally by making up song parodies. No one was around to judge me, so why not? It'd been a long time, and I realized how much I missed trying to think of the perfect words to go with the right song to fit the mood. Deep Purple's classic "Smoke on the Water" came to mind, and I immediately converted the lyrics to: "Snakes on the hay bales, one wrapped in the tines."

The time went by fast, and I killed as many snakes as I could, tossing them into a pile. I don't like killing things, but I was going to need a dead snake pile to show the impact of my efforts. I knew he didn't like snakes, either, so this extra proof of courage and bravery would earn me even more credit. This would make him realize his daughter was safe with me; that I had what it took to protect her from anything.

"Hey, get out of there!" I yelled as two dogs came out of nowhere and started messing with my snake pile. They ran off with dead snakes in their mouths and then came back empty-mouthed and took more. I was not planning on doing anything with those snakes, but the bigger the pile, the more impressed my father-in-law would be, and the darn dogs were taking some of that away. At least they left about twenty of them, but it would be a far cry from the amount of credit I deserved.

Those first few years of marriage were critical in proving to others and myself that I had what it took. I wished I could truly internalize my okay-ness and really believe people when they told me they loved me. But somewhere along the line I picked up a belief that love had to be continually earned or those who you loved would just drop you off, say goodbye, and drive off in their Mustang, never to be heard from again. I worked too hard, gave up too much I had been passionate about, and had been too lucky to let myself take people's love for granted and risk losing any of it.

Because I really had been lucky. I was married to the love of my life who I had known since elementary school and who, for some reason, said yes to me when I asked her to first go out and then marry me. Tracy's parents, sister, and extended family on both sides had only shown love and acceptance.

Tracy and I were so happy together. Within a few years of getting married, we finished our degrees and were working at the same company. I was gaining the respect of my colleagues and management, finally getting that first actuarial position. Tracy was crushing her job and had built several great work friendships.

Our life was going great, and we wanted to take the next step of having kids. I had a long road of actuarial exams in front of me, but we didn't want to wait too long as there was no guarantee of anything. We were going to try to get pregnant!

I was so excited, and I pretended I wasn't scared to death. I would work hard to be a great dad, but would I be good enough? I mean, there are a lot of terrible dads out there, and I bet a bunch of them went into parenting thinking they were going to be great dads. I prayed I had what it took, but yeah, I was excited.

CHAPTER 6:

CAN I GET THREE KIDS AND A SIDE OF VALIDATION?

———

"Let's get the team in here, stat! Mr. Fredlund, I need you to come with me into the hallway."

Seven more members of the medical staff streamed into the room where our son Christopher had just been born. His twin brother Ryan was supposed to be right behind him, but something went wrong. The doctor was trying to get me out of the room and into the hallway. "No!" I scared myself a bit with the conviction in my voice. "I can't leave them!"

The calming voice of the doctor was helpful, "Mr. Fredlund, you need to come out to the hallway with me right now, please. They are taking great care of Tracy, but I need to talk with you about our options."

As the doctor calmly guided me toward the hallway, I let Tracy's hand slip through my fingers, and I lost sight of her as the door closed behind us. "What? What is it? What is going on?" My eyes stayed on the door that led back to where my wife and son were going through something I couldn't yet comprehend.

"I need you to make a decision. Ryan is breech, and there is a risk the umbilical cord could wrap around his neck as we try to turn him. We can continue what we are doing to deliver naturally, but there is a risk things could go really wrong. The other option is we do an emergency cesarean section. It's a significant surgery, but it will ensure both baby and mom are safe. What do you want to do?"

I didn't feel equipped to answer this huge question, but I knew I must. Asking myself what Tracy would want me to do made the decision very easy. "Let's do the C-section."

"Great. We just need a couple of signatures." The doctor went back into the room, and for a moment I saw a flash of Tracy as the door opened and closed. The hospital administrator had the clipboard, papers, and pen ready to go.

"Where do I sign?" She pointed on the top page, and I scribbled like a celebrity doing a book signing. She didn't seem to care how sloppy it was. She flipped each page and pointed where she wanted me to scribble. I had no idea what I was signing. I just needed to get back into that room.

With the final page came the administrator's thumbs up, and I was back in the room. An impressive team rallied around Tracy to get baby Ryan. It was hard to stay out of the way and still hold Tracy's now-limp hand. If there was any chance she could feel my hand or my energy or my love or anything, I needed to stay connected. I tried to look away as they coated her stomach with different colored liquids and started slicing through the layers to get to our son, but

I couldn't. *There he is!* He was wiggling away underneath whatever part of the body that was.

"Don't be scared, Ryan. We've almost got you, buddy," I said under my breath with my voice cracking.

Within moments the doctors and nurses were smiling, and it was clear everything was going to be okay with Ryan. My attention shifted to Tracy, who had been through so much. I knew the surgery was rough, and she was going to be in pain. I hoped she thought I made the right decision.

"Is she okay?"

"Yes, Tracy is fine. She will be out for a while and will be sore from the surgery, but all her signs look great. Congratulations, Mr. Fredlund." I buckled over, feeling a blend of excitement, relief, love, concern, gratitude, pride, joy, stress, and amazement. I was crying and unsure which emotion created the tears—maybe all of them. "Are you okay, Mr. Fredlund?"

"Yes, I'm great. Thank you. Thank you." I'm not much of a hugger, but everyone in the room got one that day.

With each hug came another, "Congratulations, Mr. Fredlund." They kept calling me Mr. Fredlund, and it was making me feel old and oddly important at twenty-six.

From that first day, I was head over heels in love with those two boys. It was fun to see the entire family thoroughly enjoying them and how they so quickly showed different dispositions.

Hopefully, I could be the kind of dad they needed. I would read to them at night, feed them the right food, make sure the formula was the right temperature, and try to be the kind of dad they would be proud to have. I wanted them to know how much I loved them and would always be there for them, and they would never have to worry that someday I would drive away and never see them again. In time it would be fun to be their friend. I was jealous my boys would have the kind of dad I always wanted. I needed to be a good dad, not just for them but for my own validation that I was okay.

Not only did I love being a dad, I loved telling people I was a dad. I was quick to share pictures and always ready for another story. But over those first three years, I found myself getting more exhausted under the weight of growing responsibilities. Having two toddlers brings challenges, and although Tracy handled most of them, there was certainly less sleep involved for both of us.

Being a dad didn't slow down my effort to get through actuarial exams, do a great job at work, and start contributing to leadership roles at church. The validation I got at home, work, and church was fueling me like a drug. Every thank you and congratulations and smile I received was a boost that helped me keep going, giving me energy to complete another task and carry out another commitment. I was sure things would get easier once we settled into our new house, I finished the actuarial exams, and the kids got older. *I just need to get through the next five or ten years, and then things will be good.*

Most adults are incredibly busy. It's the first word we use to describe our lives. It's like a badge of honor. I was busy, too, but I think I had a different motivation. When I thought about it, I didn't want to be so busy. I really didn't. But if I wasn't, would I be judged as lazy? Would people think I wasn't doing enough? I was so concerned about what other people thought that I did things I didn't even want to do.

I wondered if my need for validation was healthy as I started to understand the depth of my dependence. I would do anything for people if they just told me they appreciated it, or even better that they appreciated me. Even though I was swamped, I would spend an afternoon helping somebody move if they just told me how much they appreciated it. I would chair the board of directors if it was shared publicly the importance of my role and how much value I added. I would volunteer to do a fundraising project at work if I thought my bosses would be impressed.

By the summer of 1999, I depended on external validation to get me through my full-time job, the long daily commute, increasing responsibilities at church, two-year-old twin boys, moving into our new house, and the upcoming birth of our daughter just a couple months away. I took great pride in comments from coworkers like, "You are so productive!" or from family members, "How do you do it all?"

I knew I was too busy. I really did. But people seemed to really appreciate and value all the things I could do, especially at work. I discovered an amazing correlation between how much I worked and produced and how much I got paid. And when push comes to shove, that's the ultimate validation, isn't it?

I had to make a few slight adjustments to my personal social schedule to accommodate my increasing responsibilities. I was no longer in a bowling league, and I gave up golfing and fantasy football. I enjoyed them, but they no longer fit into my life focused on family, career, and important volunteer work. Truth be told, I wasn't that good at those things anyway.

Our daughter, Annie, had a much less dramatic entrance into the world. For the first time, Tracy could hold one of her children right away. Tears flowed down my cheeks watching Tracy with Annie and then when her three-year-old brothers met her for the first time. They were so sweet to her.

I was so tired, but I was also so grateful. Only eight years before, I was a single college kid uncertain of my future. I wasn't even sure I had what it took to make it in this world as an adult. Now, I worked for a Fortune 500 company, and I was a husband and father of three.

I knew I could still screw this up because pride usually comes before the fall, but if I stayed humble, stayed focused, and continued to do the right things, I might even expand my success story. I doubled down on my internal commitment to be the husband and father my family needed, the businessman my company expected, and the volunteer my community thought I should be.

Months and years continued to fly by. Tracy was getting more beautiful, the kids kept growing, my job responsibilities had more impact, and my church leadership was increasing. On paper, my life was so impressive. *But how am I now thirty-four years old?* It dawned on me it'd already been four years since the Y2K scare. *What is happening? People warned me not to blink because time would fly, and wow, they were right. How can it be possible that our boys are eight and our daughter five, and that we've been married thirteen years? Shouldn't I have more memories?*

I knew I was having a huge impact in so many ways, but was I going to be this busy for the rest of my life? But if I gave something up, I wouldn't be as important. I wouldn't have the same level of impact I was having then. People wouldn't be as impressed with me. I didn't see another path other than pressing forward as an amazing provider, corporate contributor, and church leader.

Don't get me wrong, it was a good life. I enjoyed being a dad and a husband. We had fun playing games with family and friends, going out to eat, and all that. It wasn't that life was bad. It was just every so often a wave hit me, and I wondered if I was doing it right.

If external validation was the measuring stick, everything was fine, but something was starting to feel a bit off. Every time I asked Tracy, she assured me things were good with her and with the kids, but I thought something was off. I think I secretly wanted her to say, "No. You need to scale back on work or church or other stuff you are doing. You need to quit worrying so much about what other people think of you."

I was a people pleaser turned validation addict throwing out lifelines, but I was too good at hiding how I really felt. I needed someone to see through the facade and recognize what was happening inside me. But I was too deep into my own dependence to realize it. All I could tell was that something seemed off.

My mind needed a distraction during my commute home, so I flipped on the oldies station and started singing my concerns away. "Oh my gosh!" The words flew out of my mouth unexpectedly as Genesis's song "That's All" came on. One of the last parodies I wrote, which was also one of my favorites, was to that song. I called it "Dean's Hall," and it was all about our middle school janitor. I hadn't thought about that in so long.

My mind flooded with memories of the basement typewriter and working hard to get the new "Weird Al" cassette. In a moment I remembered waiting for our house to empty so I could crank up my stereo and perform without fear of anyone hearing me. I also remembered my lip sync contests in college. I used to love creatively using music to make people laugh.

As the song ended on the radio, they announced that Christopher Reeve, who played Superman, passed away at the age of fifty-two. *Wait, Superman is dead? I know he's just an actor, but still, if Superman can die, what does that mean for me?* For the first time as an adult, I was confronted with my mortality.

Logically, I knew I could die, but it never really dawned on me this way before. *Am I doing things right? Should I be spending more time at home? Should I quit the church position? Should I reduce my hours at work? Or should I do the opposite to have a greater impact in the world, to leave a greater legacy, with the time I have left?* I was more confused than anything.

That night I held my family just a little bit closer to buoy my insecurity as I pondered the right way to live. Their affection made me feel so good because they had no idea how important I was to my company or the church. In fact, they probably couldn't care less how important I was or the impact I had. They just seemed to like having me around.

Whenever I had the energy, our nightly tradition was having all three kids lie in bed with me, hanging on every word my creative brain could come up with to form a story that involved the random animals I let them choose. That night, I let them all choose an extra one, so they each got three. It's hard to create a story and keep track of nine different animals and their role in the story, but our imaginations took us through amazing adventures on boats and in forests. The story was a nice momentary escape from wondering if I measured up.

These moments nourished my soul, and I took comfort in feeling like this was the kind of thing good parents did. It was fun to just laugh and be creative and be goofy. It was such a far cry from the rest of my serious life of work, study, and responsibility. This was such a safe and sweet space, and I could almost hear Tracy smiling from the next room as she was curled up under a blanket with a good book, listening to us giggle.

CHAPTER 7:

FILLING UP
THE FREE TIME
I FINALLY EARNED

———

"Are you sure you are doing it right? Try it again!" Tracy could be persistent when she was excited about something.

"Okay, okay. I have to hang up so I can try again." I had a company-issued Blackberry, which allowed me to make phone calls when not in the office or at my desk, even from the Isanti County Fairgrounds where I was that day. I was volunteering at a booth but distracted, as I needed to get through to the automated hotline for the Society of Actuaries exam results. They posted the scores at 3:00 p.m., but too many people were trying to call right then, so I could only rely on luck. At 3:02 p.m. I still couldn't get through. Tracy was lying at home on the couch with strep throat, which meant she had all the time in the world to keep her mind fixated on whether I passed. While I wasn't happy she was unwell, I sort of wished she was busy at work because her nervousness was making me more nervous. She kept calling, and I knew it was not the right thing to do, but I ignored her so I could keep calling the hotline.

The hotline was the latest and greatest process for the exam scores that up until the year before were mailed out, which added to the already excruciating six-week wait time. The fear was the same this time of year, but now it just came with a phone call rather than opening an envelope and hoping for a score of six or higher. Anything less and I would have to retake the test in a year, usually after another three hundred hours of studying, and even then pass rates were usually under 40 percent.

Three more busy signals, and then, at 3:04 p.m., two rings and the automated voice, "Please enter your candidate number." I'd memorized it, so I entered it into the Blackberry, trying to keep my fingers from shaking: three-eight-five-zero-nine-two-one. In the slowest automated voice I had ever heard, it responded, "Candidate number three-eight-five-zero-nine-two-one. Press one if that is correct. Press two to reenter your candidate number. Press three to return to the main menu. Press zero to talk to the operator." *Seriously, I can't press one until you give me all the options? Talk faster, you dumb computer.* Finally, I pressed the number one.

The system didn't rip off the Band-Aid. Instead, it tore out every hair one at a time. "Candidate number three-eight-five-zero-nine-two-one. Stephen Fredlund. Actuarial exam: eight. Finance and enterprise risk management... Pass." *Wait, no way! Calm down, let's make sure that's right.* "To repeat this message, press one." Yeah, it was right.

Tears streamed down my face as I hung up the phone on my way out of the pole barn. My walk through the crowd of fair-goers was awkward as I knew so many of those people, and they had no idea of the life-changing phone call I just made. We did the country head nod and two-finger salute to acknowledge each other, but that was all I had energy for.

The horse barns were empty that time of day, so I started walking that direction trying to have as much privacy as possible. A few people were in there, so I went around to the back. I sat on a hay bale and let a river of tears flow. I had poured around eight thousand hours into studying for those exams over nearly a decade, spending late nights and early mornings when my eyes could barely stay open. My books were stained with baby formula, applesauce, Dr. Pepper, and drippings of winter nosebleeds. *It's over. It's really over.* During the past decade I nearly quit three times, but each time somebody in my life reminded me to stay the course. I knew the right thing to do was to persevere; to not have to tell anyone I didn't have what it took. And look at that—I did have what it took.

Finally composed, I was ready to call Tracy, who had been trying my phone nonstop for several minutes. She was as invested in this moment as I was. I started typing her number when she called again. I didn't say, "Hello," but instead answered with two words I will never forget: "I passed."

"You passed? Wait, *you passed*? Oh my god! Are you kidding? Are you sure? Could it be a mistake?" I'd never heard her ask so many questions that didn't need an answer. By this point she was screaming on the phone, and I was pretty sure she'd started crying too. I started laughing and couldn't stop. We were both relieved and ecstatic in our own ways over this very positive news.

"Yeah, it's over." All I had left to do was fly to Atlanta, sit through a bit of training, and then I would be a Fellow of the Society of Actuaries. Steve Fredlund, FSA. I couldn't believe it.

In the weeks that followed, I was congratulated by my coworkers, bosses, family, and friends. "I knew you could do it!" was the common theme. Well, they were more confident than I was. I felt sad so many of the hours came at the expense of time with Tracy and the kids, but this was a big step to having the kind of financially stable life I wanted for all of us. I proved to myself that I could be the provider I wanted to be. I showed the world what a kid from humble beginnings could do with the right mindset and commitment.

Like a bolt of lightning, studying was over, and my schedule freed up. Finally, I could take a breath, or at least a bit of time to figure out what the right thing to do was with all my extra time. But it seemed like other people became aware of my newfound capacity.

It'd only been two weeks since finding out I passed the exam when I got a knock on my office door. I was deep in a complex spreadsheet. I slowly finished a formula I was building and looked up casually to see the chief financial officer. *Holy crap! What is he doing here?* "Hey, Steve."

"Oh, hey." I stood. "How are you?" I didn't have a guest chair in my office. Actuaries don't get many visitors, and at my level I didn't have ad hoc meetings in my office. I crossed over to him at the door extending my hand, which he accepted. *Why the hell did I shake his hand? I'm so weird. Be cool. Just chill out. Oh my gosh, I'm so awkward. Does he notice me sweating? I'm really sweating. Please go away, but first tell me why you are here. I'm confused. Be cool. Stop, Steve. Just Stop.* My mind was tangled while trying to present a cool exterior.

"Congratulations on getting your FSA," he said in a voice that sounded like a true leader.

"Well, it's not official yet, but at least the exams are done." I couldn't shut off the self-talk. *Good grief, Steve. The CFO just congratulated you on a big milestone, and you deflect it? Actuaries are not timid like that. You must be confident if you want the big wigs to respect you. Okay, now, come on. You can still save this.* "Thanks, that means a lot."

"I have a research project, and I think you are the right person for it. I have already talked to your boss, and he is on board with releasing you for the project if you want it. We want to sell riders for our variable annuities, but they have way too much market risk. We need to figure out a cost-effective way to mitigate the risk before I will sign off on selling them. I need someone to figure out the best way to do this and make a recommendation to the board. What do you think?"

"It sounds fascinating, and I am definitely interested." I was trying to project confidence and professionalism while inside I already recognized this was a big career opportunity. It felt like I should say more than just that. "You said my boss is already on board?" *Yes, you dummy, he already said that.*

"Yes. It's yours if you want it." He had a smile I trusted but with just a little twist that made me wonder if a joke was coming next.

"I would love the opportunity. Thank you. I will make sure everything is in place here so we don't lose momentum with any of my current projects. What are the next steps?" *Yes, Steve. Now* that's *how an executive speaks.*

"I will have my admin set up some time for us to start discussing the details, and then I'll connect you with the product team. It will take a lot of initiative, but this is a huge opportunity for the future of the company." He finished his thought and offered me a second handshake, which made me feel better about offering a handshake earlier.

"Thank you, sir."

For me, this was about more than just the project. All my efforts at work and in studying were being recognized. I had felt affirmed through my annual reviews and the words of my bosses, but this was true validation. They would have never given me this project if they didn't think I was a great actuary. The buzz I got from this project assignment surpassed anything I'd experienced before. It was intoxicating and raised the bar for every future validation I would look for. The days of being affirmed for just doing well or making a solid contribution were over. I was now chasing the high that came with major assignments and significant impact. I knew I could change the world, and I was looking for people to trust me to do so.

For the following year, I was swamped with researching, analyzing, running models, and connecting with industry professionals. Some days I wasn't sure what I was doing; I felt like a bit of an imposter. But if the CFO thought I was the right person for the job, I must have been. He was so successful and had led the financial wing of the company so well, so he must've known what he was doing. I loved learning and solving this incredibly complex problem.

The eyes of my colleagues, boss, executives, and board were upon me and the status of my research. They were desperate for an effective risk management strategy so we could sell these special products, and they would not be disappointed. The board accepted my research and proposal and asked me to lead this brand-new department. The culmination of my hard work was a promotion and leadership position, providing me with that next-level validation I'd started to crave.

But it didn't stop there. My efforts were rewarded beyond the new position in a way I never expected. Tracy and I were sitting in a reserved waiting area with drinks and a fireplace, waiting to board a private jet with the CEO and CFO and both of their wives. The six of us were flying to San Antonio as a congratulations trip for those selected as Thrivent employees of the year. I won this honor for my analysis and recommendation, which led to launching the company's first capital markets hedging program, the one I was asked to lead. The experience with the executives and their spouses, along with the other nominees and their guests, in San Antonio was remarkable. Everything was paid for as we enjoyed great dining, custom-fitted Stetson hats, a Riverwalk cruise, and an authentic Texas barbeque overlooking the Alamo.

Fresh off the validation and buzz of that exciting project came another, equally important one. My charge this time was figuring out how to combine several products to optimize our client's retirement income. I got another shot of validation when they asked me to do this, followed by another shot upon success and having my name on the patent, followed by yet another shot of validation with another promotion and pay increase.

Finishing the actuarial exams seemed like a distant memory only two years prior. The free time was quickly reinvested into projects that created millions of dollars of value for the company, and the rest of the insurance industry was paying attention. Job offers started coming in from competitors. There is no greater shot of validation than having a "Hollywood moment" when a competitor writes a number on a piece of paper, turns it over, and slides it across the table.

I gained a lot of confidence from these experiences, but I also started looking to do more than just make small contributions to causes. In every area of my life, I started looking for ways to have a transformational impact.

At church, I moved from volunteering with drama and Sunday school to a position on the board, ultimately becoming the chair. I also agreed to a commission for two years to help start a new church in a nearby community, doing everything we could to successfully reach the people of that city. For more than a year, every Sunday morning involved picking up another volunteer and a bunch of drums followed by a stop to get a trailer out of storage before driving to another city to bring everything in and set up for church. After services, we reversed the entire process. This commitment was more than eleven hours each Sunday and one hundred miles every week. It was grueling, especially in the winter, but people were so appreciative and encouraging, and I was regularly reminded by the leadership that God was pleased with my investment of time, talent, and treasure.

In the middle of everything else happening at work, I got a visit from our chief investment officer who said he saw great potential in me to become a future C-level leader. He was authorized to have Thrivent cover the entire cost of a Master's in Business Administration at the Carlson School at the University of Minnesota. This was a $90,000 program I could go through for free. I took a deep breath. The program looked great, but it was intense and would interfere with my church board commitments. I shared the conflict, which he didn't really understand but agreed to a partial payment for a different MBA program that would better meet my schedule.

Within three years, I saw exponential growth in my corporate career and church leadership, but I wanted to make sure I still got it right when it concerned my family. It was common for me to ask Tracy, "Am I still doing okay with you and the kids? Am I spending too much time at work or church? Are you all okay?" She assured me things were good, and I knew she would tell me if they weren't. I needed reassurance from everybody I was serving, including my family, that they were happy with the level of service they were getting from me because my confidence and belief in myself depended on their level of satisfaction.

I really needed them to be okay because I was changing the world in huge ways, and with every victory, I affirmed I had what it took. With every accomplishment, influential people showed me their appreciation—more and more shots of validation. The more things I was successful at, the more people validated me, and the more I felt like I was okay.

CHAPTER 8:

BEING A CARP SOUNDS NICE

I had just started my MBA program and soon it was over. The years were churning by faster and faster, and two just passed in a blink. In another two years, I would be forty. It was hard for me to comprehend. I was proud of the life we had built and the contributions I made, but one night was spent searching the internet for ways to reduce stress. I learned a breathing technique that was supposed to help, and I was going to try it on my lunchtime walk the next day.

Andrew caught me as I was leaving the office to walk and breathe. I wish I could've told him what was really going on, but I'd already covered it with an excuse that I needed to clear my head to solve a work-related problem.

It was much colder that day, but I started my breathing exercises as soon as I stepped out the front door to head to the bridge. *Deep inhale through my nose, hold it, and then exhale.* I didn't feel any different right away, but I kept trying. My steps found a good rhythm in sync with the breathing. Out of nowhere I started singing, "I was walkin' downtown with my thick jacket, doing breathing through my nose," to the rhythm of "Our Song" by Taylor Swift.

Where did that come from? I haven't created a parody in decades and now one just magically appears. And it's Taylor Swift! I smiled, remembering how I used to spend hours writing parodies and getting so excited when I would find just the right words.

The Stone Arch Bridge is an iconic and historic marker of Minneapolis, connecting the east coast to the west long ago for trains bringing goods. I was hoping it became my bridge to bring understanding to my current confusion. My nose felt numb, and in a small way I hoped this would numb my brain too. It was hard to stay focused on a dumb breathing exercise, so I started imagining what it would feel like to physically be an exhaled breath floating and dissipating into the October sky.

Does our breath feel anything? I'd do anything right now to avoid thinking about the one thing I really need to think about. I was starting to feel unhappy far more often than I used to. Before it was about certain situations, but now it felt more like a core issue. It felt like I *was* unhappy, not just feeling unhappy about some specific thing.

But my unhappiness didn't make sense. I had a fantastic job at a great company. I was just named employee of the year and received a big promotion. I was getting paid what seemed like Monopoly money, considering my first seven years growing up in a rural town that had four houses, a bar, and a cheese plant. I had a wonderful marriage and three healthy kids. I was heavily involved in church, and I had the respect of my community. From all angles my life looked ideal, but it felt far less than.

The cold weather reduced foot traffic over the bridge that day, but it didn't slow down the carp I saw in the water below. They seemed content and were a nice distraction from how serious my problem felt. I fought with the distractions that abounded and wanted to focus on figuring this out rather than watching some damn fish swimming in a river.

I thought I only needed to listen to the voices of those who were telling me how much they appreciated the effort I had put in, or my financial contributions, or my commitment to be there for my kids. *Everyone tells me I'm great. Why don't I feel equal to their words? Why can't I just believe them? If I'm as great as they say I am, I should easily feel happy.*

I worked hard to do things right. I gave up my childish dreams about becoming the new "Weird Al" Yankovic to become a better student. I chose the right college based on what the experts told me I should do rather than chasing some fantasy that I could have been part of a huge university and their football tradition. I married the right girl, had the right number of kids, secured the right job at the right company, took on the right projects, believed the right things, volunteered doing the right things, and spent the right amount of time with my family. I had been doing everything right.

I had success and accolades while missing the essential ingredient—me. The more I gave to others the more I was feeling disconnected from myself. Quite literally, something had to give, and time would create the opportunity for it.

I also felt alone in my unhappiness. I had always been able to tell Tracy anything, and I always had great coworkers, fellow volunteers, and extended family to make me feel good about myself. But being unhappy was not something we had discussed.

I didn't want to make Tracy nervous by telling her I was struggling. For some reason I felt like if I told my manager, I would lose his respect. I figured I could tell my mom, but I would feel terrible complaining about my life to someone who worked very hard as well to provide for my brother and me. My church friends would tell me to "pray about it," which I was starting to question had any point at all, even though I had been doing it. My other friends seemed so happy and successful, so I didn't think they would understand.

Then I thought of somebody who may be able to help: Paul, a wise instructor from my MBA program. I called him, and to my surprise he answered the phone, catching me a bit off guard and flustered.

"Hey, Steve!"

"Hey, Paul. Man, it's great to hear your voice. How are you?"

He was too wise to know I wasn't calling just to check in. "I'm doing well, but how about you? What's going on?"

"Well… I'm struggling, and I'm not sure who can help." My admission felt like weakness. "Would you have some time in the next couple of weeks to chat through it?"

"Oh, I'm sorry to hear that. Let's get together today." At least he recognized the urgency, and we agreed to meet at 4:30 p.m.

I arrived a few minutes early, and there he was, of course, already waiting for me. He stood as soon as he saw me and greeted me with a big hug. "Whatever is happening, I'm sorry you are going through it. I'm honored you chose to reach out and share it with me." This simple act of kindness brought tears to my eyes as we took a seat. He realized the depth of whatever this was and said, "Whenever you are ready, Steve."

For several minutes I unloaded what I was feeling, sharing my best guess at what it was and supporting facts that might have had something to do with it. He listened carefully, taking notes and nodding his head to acknowledge he understood while at the same time encouraging me to keep sharing. Just having someone listen like that soothed my soul.

I ended my monologue, closing with a small grin to signal I was finished and my way of passively apologizing when I felt like I talked for too long. I said, "Now I'll hang up and listen."

Paul jumped right in. "Thanks for sharing all that, Steve. Do you remember doing the StrengthsFinder assessment during the MBA program?" I nodded with a quizzical look. "Good. What were your top five strengths?"

"Learner, relator, achiever, strategic, and self-assurance."

"Great. Think about the big promotion you just accepted. On a scale of one to five, how much were you leveraging each of your strengths before the promotion?" I saw where Paul was going with this. I assigned all fours and fives to the strengths.

"Great." He continued, "Now give me the ratings for each of the strengths after the promotion."

The light bulb was fully on now. "They are all ones and twos," I sheepishly admitted.

"You are grieving the loss of your strengths. Before the promotion you were operating in your giftedness, and now you are not. You are getting paid more and have more responsibility, but you are not using your strengths, and your soul is grieving because of it."

Paul was right. I never considered *not* taking the promotion. I never lined it up against my strengths. *I mean, that's the game, right? Work hard, get noticed, take promotions.* My promotion was a testament to my knowledge, skills, work ethic, and capability, but the job responsibilities were not aligned with my strengths. "Thank you so, so much. This is the breakthrough I needed." Even before he exited, my mind was racing with steps I could take.

"Let's keep in touch, Steve." I extended my hand, which he brushed aside and gave me another one of his enveloping hugs.

Paul confirmed my suspicion that I had done something wrong. I was disappointed in myself that I didn't think of this. It was so obvious. *Duh, my job changed and I'm doing stuff that's not in my wheelhouse, which has made me unhappy. How could I not figure this out? But the good news is Paul figured it out for me! Now that I know what is wrong, I can fix it and start doing things right, and that will make me happier.*

I was awake until 2:00 a.m. brainstorming all the ways I could align my life more with my strengths. It was so obvious: If I spent more time doing things aligned with my strengths, I would certainly see a positive turn in my happiness.

But rather than adjusting my responsibilities, I was struggling to see how to make the changes I needed, I decided to start looking at new things I could do that would utilize my strengths if that's what would make me happy. So many ideas came to mind, and I really enjoyed the process of brainstorming and finding a creative solution to my problem. I was excited to become happier by—wait for it—doing more.

I loved starting new things and taking on new challenges. Something about learning combined with creative problem-solving really got my juices flowing. So, adding more made complete sense although I may have strayed away from the advice Paul was really trying to give me, which was more about adjusting than adding.

Over the next year, I became a part-time executive pastor, started a nonprofit doing humanitarian work in Rwanda, and launched a poker podcast, each of which I invested a lot of time in. I enjoyed all of them, they were all aligned with my strengths, each had great impact, and I felt validated by the results. But my unhappiness continued and even got worse.

CHAPTER 9:

FINE, I ADMIT IT:
I'M MISERABLE

———

An entire decade had passed since I first became aware of my unhappiness. I had become forty-eight years old. Where did all that time go?

My life remained good, with some great times and great people, but there continued to be a secret undercurrent no one really saw. Yes, I truly had times I enjoyed, and I honestly loved Tracy and the kids, and I was grateful for what I had, and I was proud of what I accomplished. But life, for as good as it was, completely stopped feeling like it was my life.

I worked extremely hard to do everything I should, fueled by the validation received from all of it. I was getting close to fifty years old, and I was the least happy I had ever been. All the times I told myself, "In five years it will be different," had not come to fruition.

Don't get me wrong. I owned it. Clearly, I missed the mark somewhere along the line. I took great comfort in knowing I successfully tried to do everything in my power to make the lives of others happy, but apparently, I didn't know how to help myself. For ten years I had been having confusing conversations with myself. My life was good, and I was happy about that, but I didn't feel happy inside. I was pleased with the decisions, but honestly, I was feeling unfulfilled.

I was a living contradiction. I was confused. And my heart was not happy.

Tracy was asleep on the couch as I pondered life from my recliner. I finished almost an entire bag of Tostitos and a jar of salsa as I watched the Minnesota Twins limp toward the end of their 2018 season. My laptop was open, but I lacked the motivation to update my work spreadsheet, make the necessary changes to the nonprofit website, submit the board report, check email, update the latest podcast, prioritize my to-do list for the next day, edit the video, or anything else at the top of my three to-do lists.

I realized I just polished off more than one thousand calories worth of chips. I rinsed out the salsa bowl and threw away the empty chip bag. I was gaining weight, but this was not the time for discipline. I conquered the ice cream next. *I should find a better method of escape, but what's the point?*

I was so tired and dreaded going to work the next day. I didn't hate the actual work I did or my coworkers or my boss or the company, yet I was in complete dread about going. How did it come to this? These were supposed to be the years where those first inklings of unhappiness launched me on a journey back to restoring my happiness. Instead, life felt like drudgery.

I still didn't understand this unhappiness. It was worse at this point and still didn't make sense. On paper, my life was even better than it was ten years earlier. I had more accomplishments, influence, and money. So what was going on?

I created a list of everything I had been involved with the past ten years, looking for themes or correlations to my happiest times. I'd done this many times before but still found no profound clues from my effort. Still, each night I spent some time going through them to look for signs of what was happening. *I wonder if Paul is proud of how intentionally I have pursued my strength-alignment. I bet he would know what I am doing wrong, even if he is proud of me.*

I was quite deep in thought when I heard some rustling behind me. "Good night, honey," Tracy said as she started moving toward the stairs. "Honey?" she said again.

"Oh my gosh, I'm so sorry. I just have a lot on my mind." I improved my tone and said, "Good night, sweetie!" The vocal change was way too obvious, and we both recognized I was forcing myself to sound better than I really was.

She came back my way and knelt at the side of the chair. "I don't want to tell you what to do, but I really think it would help you to see a therapist."

She was right, but it killed me to think my unhappiness was causing her any concern or frankly even that she knew. "I know. I know," I told her. I realized this may sound dismissive of her, so I apologized. "I'm sorry. I appreciate that. I know that might help, but I don't know. How can they help me figure out what's wrong with me? You are probably right, but I don't know. I can't even think straight. I'm sorry."

"You don't need to be sorry, sweetie. I just want to see you happy again. I don't like it when you're not happy. It bums me out, and I'm sure the kids can tell."

Oh great, this is worse than I thought. The kids can tell. And how did she make my unhappiness about her? I'm the one suffering. I'm the one who needs help. But now it feels like the reason I should get help is so she can feel better. I knew she cared about me and had my best interest at heart, but the unhappiness and lack of confidence did some nasty things to my brain. It twisted my thoughts into anger at her for just asking me if a therapist might help. My brain gave up the battle. "I know. I'm the worst."

"You are not the worst." She seemed a little agitated. "I just want to know what will help. You must admit you're not happy. Right?" Recently she reminded me of "Old Steve," the guy she married who was filled with jokes, fun, and goofiness. She remembered when I was free and truly happy. She knew that even when I was at my happiest now days, it was a dim shadow of my former self.

I've never yelled at her, but I was a bit frustrated and felt like I wanted to. Instead, I said with force, "You are right, Tracy. All right? Is that what you want to hear? I'm frickin' miserable. Nothing is working. I've done everything I know to do to align myself with my strengths. I gave back the promotion.

I started the nonprofit. I got my MBA; worked at the church; quit the church. None of it has made me happier."

I immediately regretted saying any of that. It wasn't the right way to talk to my wife or anyone for that matter. "I'm sorry. It's just so damn frustrating. And I feel all alone because I don't want to worry you. And I feel so damn guilty because what in the world can I possibly be unhappy about? And now the kids might be noticing. I'm sorry."

"You don't need to be sorry, sweetie. I just want you to figure this out so we can have 'Old Steve' back. I want you to be honest with me. I want you to admit when you are struggling. I can handle it."

"Thanks. I'm sorry. Let me think about it." I always needed some time to process. After twenty-seven years of marriage, she knew this was my way. This was not our first rodeo.

Tracy kissed me sweetly on the forehead. "I love you more than my luggage."

It's fun having those inside jokes, and this one made me smile. "I love you too. I'll get better. I'm sorry."

As soon as she made it up the stairs, the tears started to flow. I had nothing to show for my hard work over the past ten years of trying to do everything right. Everyone around me benefited, but what did I get? I should've taken comfort knowing I used my education, privilege, and strengths to benefit my family, community, and people around the world. I should've felt proud knowing I helped build a wonderful life for my wife and kids. I did want these things for them, but what was in it for me?

That felt like a selfish question. *What's in it for me? Where did that come from?* I was ticked the universe put me in this situation where I was now asking myself selfish questions. I made an agreement with the universe I would work hard and do everything right, and in exchange it would reward me with a good life, and that would make me happy. I kept up my end of the bargain, but I was anything but happy.

Sleep didn't come easily that night. *Do I wake her up and apologize again? Do I pretend I have figured out the solution? Will there ever be a solution? If I'm not happy now, when will I ever be?* For several weeks these questions plagued me, separating me from the sleep I so desperately needed.

CHAPTER 10:

AN ACTUARY'S GOODBYE

———

"Heading in early again?" Tracy asked as she started getting up for the day. You can take the girl off the farm, but you can't take the farm out of the girl, as she was rarely in bed past 5:00 a.m.

I was still reeling from our conversation a few weeks prior where I snapped at her as I made my confession about my unhappiness. I had been more intentional about acting happier, trying to convince her I had turned a corner. I responded as chipper as I could at the butt crack of dawn, "Yep! There's a lot going on, and I want to finish some analysis so it's ready for our morning meeting."

The world of strategic workforce planning is as boring as it is complex, which meant I could say whatever I wanted, and she would just smile and wish me good luck. On this day, my response was a complete fabrication. I was going in early to have as much alone time as possible.

I had been at this company for seven years, and over that time I had seven different bosses and four significantly different positions. My annual reviews had been stellar, but it had been a whirlwind. I had just started a global role, working with a small and young, yet impressive team. Our mission was exciting, and on the surface being part of a start-up group had immediate appeal. But there was a reason I was trying to avoid being in the office with everyone else.

My work buildings came into view even earlier that day than normal. Sweat formed on my brow despite the cool morning air. I turned the air conditioner to max and cranked the fan up as far as it would go.

"Here we go again," I muttered. For two weeks I had started sweating as soon as I saw those buildings, and I didn't know what was going on. *Is this anxiety? Am I having a heart attack? What is triggering all these feelings? I just want them to stop.*

I took my exit off the highway and entered the company's parking garage. I circled my way up to the roof, even though I could just park near the door on any of the first three levels. I backed into my spot as the sweat started rolling down my face even more. The air conditioner worked great, but it was no match for what was happening in my body. I adjusted every vent to blow directly toward my face. I practiced my breathing. I was scared. *What if this never changes? What if this is my life? I have it all, and I want more, something I can't seem to find. And how is that possible when I've done all the right things all along the way?*

Could this be hormonal hot flashes? I allowed myself a brief chuckle at the idea. *My last physical didn't show anything wrong with me, but maybe they missed something.* The sweat meandered its way through my chest hair and onto my belly.

I was sweating from what felt like everywhere on my body. Marathon runners didn't sweat like this.

I convinced my hand to move toward the car door and grip the handle before it finally resisted. My fingers curled around the handle, but my brain refused to let me pull it. I was paralyzed like someone just pressed pause on my life movie. Again, I questioned what the hell was going on.

My tear ducts joined in, apparently not wanting to feel left out. The tears from my cheeks now combined with streams of sweat like rivers on my face with a current strong enough to form pools at the base of my neck. This felt humiliating and demoralizing.

I released the door handle. Opening the door was not going to happen. I needed my hands anyway to wipe my neck before my shirt was soaked. I'm sure there were already massive wet spots at my armpits, belly, and lower back. *Dammit. Stop it. How can I be sweating when I'm literally just sitting here in max air conditioning?* Then my body started to shake.

I took a deep inhale. *Hold. Deep exhale. Just breathe. It's going to be okay. No rush. You've got this.*

Everything started calming down. Tears and sweat subsided. I was going to be okay. The vents were finally starting to cool my body. I knew once I got inside, I would be able to go to the bathroom and use paper towels to dry myself off. It was still super early. All would be fine. I took one last look at my face in the rearview mirror to give myself a pep talk. "You are strong. You've got this."

Slow inhale. Deep exhale. I do, in fact, have this.

It wasn't even 6:00 a.m. as I started the long walk from the parking garage into the building. "Good morning, Bobby!" I needed the security guard to know I was okay, happy, and excited to be there. I didn't want him to suspect anything was wrong with me.

He was quick to respond. "Another early one, hey, Steve?"

"You know it! Early bird gets the worm!" Although my real answer should've been, "Early bird gets to leave early and minimize their time in the stupid open office environment."

I was comforted by my spreadsheets. They were so familiar to me and made me feel like things were normal. Sweating and crying were something I would have to figure out at some point, but as I started working on the tool I was building, I realized the impact I could have. Leaders around the world would be able to manage their people and optimize performance far more effectively. I couldn't let anything slow down my progress. My leaders were depending on me to come through.

Those first two hours were great. *It's 8:00 a.m. and still no other team members are here!* I liked all of them, but the same thing that happened in the car was happening during the day when they were all there. So, every moment by myself felt like a balm to a sunburn.

The company's management referred to the design of our workspace as an "open office" environment. There were no high walls, just some workstations with four-foot panels sharing table space inside one big open room.

Maybe if nothing was wrong with me, this would've been fun. Like I said, I really liked everyone on the team, and collectively they were dynamic, vibrant, and productive. We generated energy from each other. One team member stood at her computer repeating German words from the lessons she was taking between calls. Another walked the entire open office space, talking with prospective clients through his headset while bouncing a tennis ball in a constant rhythm of floor, wall, and catch. Our boss was a young genius who was full of energy and enjoyed playing opera vinyl records on his turntable. Did I mention we had an espresso machine people lined up to use, especially around 9:00 a.m.?

My analytical work was intense, and I found it hard to focus within that environment. My noise-canceling headphones helped only marginally. My sweat glands were automatically activated on the arrival of my coworkers. As soon as the first one showed up, every minute was painful, and the day was something I tried to tolerate. I started watching the clock, waiting for 2:30 p.m. when I could justify leaving. There were 19,800 seconds between 9:00 a.m. and 2:30 p.m., and on this day I may have counted each one.

It wouldn't be long now until the full band was assembled. Soon the *ensemble* would be playing its hours-long masterpiece of floor, wall, catch, narrated in German and with the musical score of Pavarotti and sound bursts from the espresso pump.

I sent yet another email and left yet another voicemail with my boss, his boss, my former boss, and another HR executive I trusted. "Seriously, I don't know what to do. I need my own space. I am unproductive and cannot focus with so much activity going on." No one listened or cared. The only response I got was how proud they seemed to be to have an entrepreneurial setting. I could see I had no option but to do my work in that shared space as part of the team.

I know there are human resources rules about adjusting to meet needs of specific employees, but they weren't doing that in my situation. It's ironic because I worked in HR for seven years, and they were the only group not willing to make reasonable accommodations for their employees. I knew if I were still working in the investment area, they would have worked with me to come up with a solution. I needed to figure out how to fight through it. I needed to be strong and make it work. What other option did I have?

Today was rough, but tomorrow will be better. It has to be.

The next morning started as a rerun of the day before. Leave home early, get the sweats when I see the building, start crying after parking on the ramp, yada, yada, yada. But this day became a little different. It was 5:45, the time I was usually able to pull it together in my car, but that wasn't happening this time. My fingers were still wrapped around the door handle at 6:00, and then 6:30, and then 7:00, and then 7:30.

I sent an email to the team and told them I woke up sick and I couldn't come in that morning. If I started feeling better, I would show up and join them for the second half of the day. I had so much to do, and this was the day I was going to demo one of the new tools. My boss would be disappointed, but maybe I could go in later to get him what he wanted.

Oh shoot, I can't just sit here. What if one of my teammates sees me? I drove a couple blocks away to a nearby empty lot. I gave myself a pep talk. "Come on, Steve. Pull yourself together. It's just a job. Get in there and get it done." My sweating increased, and my chest started feeling tight. *Is it normal to feel your own heartbeat? That's never happened before. Is this how I am going to die? Am I overreacting? Should I call Tracy and say goodbye just in case? Should I call 911 or drive to the hospital? Should I just lie down? Someone, please, tell me what I should do.*

Please don't let this be how it ends. This can't be how it ends. I am not going to call Tracy. I don't want to worry her if this is nothing. What would I even say? I mean, how do you say goodbye to someone forever? What if nothing happens, do you then tell them "just kidding"?

I opened the Notes app on my phone and created a message for my family, planning to leave it open on the car seat in case this was the end. I was weeping and couldn't believe I was typing this: "Tracy, Chris, Ryan, and Annie, I love you so much." I wasn't sure why I was worried about using commas and proper capitalization. Maybe they would find that amusing later. I continued typing: "Remember I have a folder in the top of the black filing cabinet in case anything happens. You know who to give it to who can help with everything." I was glad I did that although I chuckled a little bit realizing that was exactly how an actuary would say goodbye. "Here's what you need when I'm dead." In the middle of my crisis, that somehow made me smile. *I think they might find it funny after a while too.* I reclined my seat and closed my eyes.

I knew I was feeling better when I started asking myself questions. *Why didn't I call an ambulance? Why didn't I drive to a hospital?* Luckily, that was not my final day on earth. If it were, it would have been much harder to write this book. Feeling better, I deleted the note in my phone and never shared that story until now.

From my car, I emailed my HR rep and let her know what was going on. She told me the next steps I should take, which included seeing a therapist as soon as possible. I emailed Tracy to also let her know what was going on, knowing we would chat about it when she got home from work. I hoped that conversation would go okay. It was hard to explain what was happening, but I wanted her to know, though I didn't want her to worry. I expected her to be happy I was seeing a therapist, even though she was disappointed I didn't go when it was her idea. I needed to figure out the right way to tell her about this.

For the first time in my adult life, I felt vulnerable, scared, and weak, which meant I felt like I wasn't enough. *Husbands, parents, nonprofit leaders, and businessmen should be strong, like I used to be.* This was a dark time for me, and I refused to let anyone realize how dark it really was. My goal was to get through it and never let people know how bad it was. That seemed like the right approach.

I was going to work hard to understand what I was going through before I got to the therapist. I wanted to optimize our time together. I was skeptical she would be able to help, but who knew. At that point, I would try anything.

CHAPTER 11:

THE QUESTION
THAT CHANGED EVERYTHING

———

I have always loved solving problems. Apparently, it is in my nature. However, I don't like being stumped, and only twenty minutes into my first session with the therapist, she had me stumped. I shared my story and why I thought I needed help when she interrupted me. "Let me ask you this. What kind of life do you want to have?"

Her question left me confused. *What kind of life do I want to have?* As I searched for an answer, my mind connected to a similar question I was asked some ten years earlier, "What kind of African safari do you want to have?" The guide was helping me create a safari experience for our group and asked me this very question. *Aren't all safaris the same? Isn't it always Jeeps, acacia trees, elephants, zebras, and lions?*

With a bewildered face, I responded to the guide, "I guess we want the African safari kind of African safari."

He laughed. "You are thinking of the default safari. It's what most people think of, but there are many more. You can canoe next to hippos, take nighttime voyages looking for

Nile crocodiles, hang out with mountain gorillas, take a hot air balloon ride, bungee jump, track migration, and more."

"Steve? Did you hear my question?" My therapist brought me back to her office. She was staring at me, patiently waiting for an answer.

"Um, yeah. What kind of life do I want, right? I don't know. I guess I want a good life."

She probed deeper. "For the past twenty minutes you have tried to explain why you were crying in your car by sharing your story and struggles. You shared about trying to do things right and to meet the expectations of those around you. You talk a lot about what you should and shouldn't do."

I nodded and tried desperately to figure out where she was going with this and what it had to do with telling her about the kind of life I wanted. She continued, "I would like to have you try something. Take away what you think you should do, or what others think you should do, or what people expect you to do. Get to the point where it's just you. What kind of life do you want to have?"

I searched my brain for any answer she might be okay with.

Tracy wanted our life to have financial stability, which I wanted too. I guess financial stability was the life I wanted. My boss wanted me to become a strategic workforce planning expert, which sounded good because I liked learning new things. So maybe the life I wanted was also filled with learning new things. But wait, so many people assured me the nonprofit work I was doing in Rwanda was changing the world, so I guess the life I wanted was one of transformational impact. I guess Rwanda felt like the front runner for me.

I must confess I miss laughing and joking around like I used to, but who does that help? I should probably say something about leadership because I know the world needs great leaders, and I've been told I have what it takes.

Wait. Duh, I forgot about being a husband and dad. Whoa, that was close. I want a life where I am a great husband and dad. I want them to know I am there for them no matter what. I want my wife to be happy she married me and the kids to be glad I am their dad.

What did she ask me again? Oh, right, take away what other people expect or what I think I should do. My mind wondered about how to solve this. How would I separate the two? I wanted people to like and accept me and to tell me I'm okay because that's how I could feel good about myself. So, I wanted the kind of life that led to people liking, accepting, and validating me.

I was lost in my own mind. *What do I want? I want to be happy, but I can't just declare what I want and, poof, there it is. I want to feel okay about myself, which means making other people happy.* I was spiraling. *Maybe this is a trick question. Maybe I am supposed to answer that life focused on myself is selfish, and that the right thing to do is what I'm doing now, thinking about what everyone else wants or expects or feels like I should do, and then morphing to become who they need me to be because that is the ultimate act of service and selflessness. No, that can't be it. She would have asked me a different question.*

"Steve? Do you understand the question?"

"Yeah, I'm just thinking." *What does she want to hear? Is she expecting me to have a good answer, or is she expecting me to not really know? Are other people honestly able to answer this? Why don't I have an answer? Should I make up an answer or tell her I don't have the first clue? What is the right answer? Think, Steve, think! What kind of life do I really want?* I desperately searched every nook and cranny of my brain, like I was late to a meeting and couldn't find my car keys.

"Steve?" she tried again.

I tried humor. "Oh, did you want an answer now?" I chuckled to reinforce how funny my comment was, but she was not having it. She sat calmly, looking at me and waiting. At this point I figured out the answer, but I wasn't sure I had the guts to share it. *But what's the point of going to therapy if I'm not going to share?* My vocal cords translated the truth in my brain into English, and I was able to open my lips just enough for the words to slip through.

"What was that?" she insisted.

Ugh. Fine. Whatever. Frustrated, I let her have it. "I have no idea. There, are you happy? I admit it. I have no idea." This was perhaps the most honest I had been in my first forty-eight years of life, but I regretted my tone. "I'm sorry. I'm sorry. I didn't mean to yell at you."

"You have nothing to apologize for. I'm glad you got emotional about this." I felt better because I didn't want her upset with me.

She explained I was a people pleaser, even more so than most Minnesotans. She figured some things from my youth contributed to my desperate need to have people like me. Maybe people left me or otherwise disappointed me, which I had interpreted as something I did wrong. I thought of the list I made just five years prior of those who have disappointed me, thinking about what I might have done to lead to their actions. The list represented a lot of pain and self-reflection but ultimately made me feel like a victim, which was certainly not what strong people were.

She shared how deeply I connected my disappointment from others with something I must have done. This was why in the past it became critical for me to gain validation of those around me, not only a one-time endorsement but the need for continuous validation. I smiled and nodded, letting her know she was on the right track. I thought of how often our daughter made fun of me for asking Tracy if she was okay. I mean, I would ask her out of the clear blue, sometimes multiple times in a day. I needed to know if she was okay because if she wasn't okay, I wasn't okay. If I helped her become okay, then by association I was okay also.

She also explained the mastery I had in meeting the needs and wants of others. Not only did I have the skill, but I took the initiative to identify problems, come up with creative solutions, and then execute strategies to get the results they wanted. For decades, this created opportunities for me to lead projects, manage people, make more money, and earn the respect of my peers and leaders.

She could tell I was processing. "What do you think, Steve?"

I couldn't believe she had these insights from what I shared. I started to see for the first time somebody was helping me like I had helped others in the past. "I'm going to need a minute." Her body language suggested I could take all the time I needed.

As the minutes passed, I became increasingly hopeful there may be an explanation, even if it was some sort of victim mentality or addiction to the validation of others. My brain was mush.

"I'm completely overwhelmed by all you have said. Can we end early and talk about this next time? I need more time to think about all of this. Is that okay?"

We both realized the irony of my last question at the same time. She smiled "Do you need me to be okay with it?" I gave her a fist bump. *What am I doing? What am I, twelve years old?* But she gave one back, and it turned out to be a great way to end our first session. "Let's chat at the same time Friday."

For two days I ruminated on her insights. I had spent ten years trying to figure out what was wrong with me, and twenty minutes into our first session she pinpointed the issue. Was that even possible? History told me it might be. I was reminded of my first appointment with an orthopedic surgeon who figured out what was causing my knee dislocations after a decade of confusion.

If she is right, maybe we can find a solution although I don't necessarily love what it means about my past. It explains why I have worked so hard in helping others, why I am so crushed when my efforts are under-appreciated or receive negative feedback, why social media trolls cause me to lose sleep for weeks, why I end friendships when I feel like they are one sided, and maybe even why I leave communities when I can no longer serve as their leader.

Could it be my generosity has been driven by an inflated need for external validation? Is this why I did humanitarian work in Africa? Am I even passionate about clean water and malnutrition and lack of education? Bring me a trombone. I need to throw up!

Is this why I have such high expectations for how people will respond when I help them? Is it why I get frustrated when people don't seem grateful enough? Is this why I am frustrated when people don't show the same level of interest in my life as I do in theirs? Am I only asking them questions because I crave their attention in return?

Brain, please stop.

The more questions I asked, the more I thought she was right and the worse I felt. I needed the truth, but maybe I couldn't handle the truth.

Is this why I offer to run to the store for Tracy late at night? Or haul boxes for people because it's "on my way"? Or accept meeting requests from people who could use my help even if I'm completely swamped? Am I truly passionate about helping people or simply recognize that is how I will get the next fix of validation I now know I crave?

Why don't people go out of their way to help me in the same way I do for them? These ingrates continue accepting what I offer but don't offer anything in return. I mean, sure, I tell them I don't want anything in return, but they should know that is just a Minnesota nice lie, and I expect they'll help me when I need it without me asking. Why am I nice to people at all?

For two days, around the clock, these questions swirled wildly in my brain. I felt a wide array of things including shame, embarrassment, sadness, loneliness, and worse, afraid I could not overcome it.

"Hey, Steve. Welcome back," my therapist said with a polite smile and first bump as I cracked a smile and took a seat. "Have you had a chance to think about our last conversation?"

I chuckled briefly. "It's literally all I have been doing. I think you are right, but…" my voice cracked, "…but if you are right, I feel so ashamed. I feel like so much of my life has been a lie; that I've thought I was this selfless guy, but ultimately I am deeply selfish, helping people just so I can feel better about myself when they thank me."

She assured me even though I might have become dependent on validation, it didn't mean my core being was not a good person or that I was completely selfish. She had a way of pulling me out of the death spiral of my brain and grounding me in a place where I felt like I was okay, which we had established was important to me.

I had a burning question to ask her. "So if this has been a lifelong issue, why was it triggered now with such a strong physical and emotional reaction?"

"More than likely, you lost sources of validation you were depending on. Have there been any changes that might have caused this?"

Is she clairvoyant or a stalker or just incredibly good at what she does? There had been quite a few changes, some I initiated and others that happened outside of my control. Over our next few sessions, we dug into the details about a number of these changes.

The obvious one was my job. For twenty-five years I had been in corporate roles, with most of that in Fortune 500 companies. It'd only been a few weeks, but I hadn't been at work since the breakdown in my car outside my job. Leaving like I did made me feel like I lost credibility with my coworkers, boss, and executives, even though my core issue was something any other analytic would understand. I didn't know any actuary who would survive an open office environment with a tennis-ball-bouncing, German-learning, opera-music-listening, espresso-making team. But the greater reason could be I no longer had a boss, colleagues, coworkers, and friends in the corporate world to encourage and validate me.

Six months prior, my nonprofit efforts resulted in our core project becoming fully funded well ahead of schedule. This was incredibly exciting. We took four trips and raised more than three million dollars, more than three times our long-term goal. The impact had been staggering, and they now had the funds they needed to complete the community transformation to self-sustainability. This meant we would stop trying to raise more funds, but it also meant our partner organization would no longer partner with us for more trips to Rwanda. Of course, I was proud of the work we had done and thrilled for the people of Kivuruga, but it was the end of our ten-year effort. No more events. No more guest speaking to raise awareness. No more meeting new volunteers or donors. No more gathering homemade dresses or rain boots or school supplies to bring with us. No more trip teams. No more newspaper articles or radio appearances.

A couple of years prior, I dropped out of the church scene. This was motivated by questions about my faith that led to a complete deconstruction and reconstruction of what I believed, and the result was losing the community of people who were constantly validating me (at least, most of them). I was an executive pastor who served on several boards, led many volunteer efforts, preached dozens of times, led adult Sunday school classes, and helped start other churches. With so many people with so many good things to say about me, it was a validation addict's dream.

Oh, and about a month prior, our youngest moved away to college. Annie had always been so encouraging, and now she wasn't around to make me feel okay as a dad and as a human. She texted a lot, but it wasn't the same. This also happened when Ryan left home, but I had so many other sources of validation it didn't have the same impact.

After all this processing, she hit the mark again by stating, "If I am right that the validation of others is a key driver of you feeling okay about yourself, then the changes over the last couple years have thrown you into serious withdrawal, just like an addict who can't get their fix. I'm guessing you have started looking for more validation from those who are left, primarily Tracy."

"Um, yeah, that's exactly what's happening." I was now trying to build my own business, doing coaching and consulting, and I kept running stuff past Tracy. She wasn't an entrepreneur or a small business owner or a coach or a consultant. She tried to be supportive, but she didn't really get what I was sharing or looking for. And because of that, her responses had not felt like the support I was looking for and, maybe more honestly, craving. I put her in a no-win situation, and I hadn't realized it until right then.

At my lowest point, I felt a ray of hope. If we knew what the problem was, maybe we could fix it. I was struggling, but for the first time in a long time, I was optimistic.

CHAPTER 12:

THE SAFARI DUDE EMERGES

I was going through validation withdrawal, and it was brutal. Worse was realizing the reason I was unhappy was because not enough people were telling me I was okay. How ridiculous was that? I never considered myself needy, but apparently I was. At least my neediness was more covert because it was hidden underneath the cover of my kindness, generosity, and intelligence.

The day of my final scheduled meeting with my therapist came. My insurance wouldn't cover more sessions, but we'd made good progress, and I thought I got what I needed and was ready to move on. I was going to miss the comfort of her chair and insight and the oddly soothing watercolor paintings scattered about her office. Although my addiction was nothing that would make the news or cause family controversy, it helped to know she was sworn to confidentiality.

She had been a great advocate skilled in taking our conversations and boiling it down to what I needed to know. I had one burning question before we finished our time together: "How do I stop needing people to validate me?"

"That's an important question, but I don't think it's the next thing for you to worry about. In fact, you may never shake the need for external validation. Plus, there is a healthy need in humans to be validated, so your life may be about knowing the difference between healthy validation and the other kind that brought you to me."

That wasn't a promising start to our final session. She went on to explain all the validation I lost over the last year had brought me to the breaking point, but the core underlying issue was that the validation I depended on was tied to stuff I wasn't personally passionate about. So much of what I was doing started with what people needed, and then I'd insert myself into the situation to be the solution. People really appreciated me doing this, flooding me with gratitude and accolades. And even though I cared about the things I was doing, ultimately, I cared more about the validation they brought, and I wanted more.

She shared another important insight. "When you start with what other people expect of you, you are dependent on them to validate you. When you start with what you want, you give yourself a chance to find validation within. And given who you are, you will also find external validation no matter what you do."

I took notes because I didn't trust my memory, and I was using a notebook just like I used to keep stats. I had even structured my notes in the same way, creating sections with my pencil for the different categories. I just added an entry for "Next steps: Focus on what I enjoy rather than what people need" and for "Key insights: The right people will validate me no matter what I do."

I mean, if she was right, the formula was easy. Do what I enjoy and trust that validation will follow. But that's the challenge—overcoming the years of experience and relationships that encouraged doing the "right" things and conveniently defined what those were—isn't it?

So, what do I enjoy? I wanted to start listening to my own heart, assuming I could still hear it. In a world filled with others telling me what the right thing was I should be doing, it was time I defined my own path forward, even if it was unright in their eyes. My mind went back to the first question the therapist asked me, "What kind of life do you want to have?" Could it be as easy as figuring that out and intentionally going after it?

She encouraged me to try this in small ways at first; to do something I enjoyed that was not lined up with what I used to think was the right thing. She challenged me to notice what it felt like, letting me know it would lead to greater empowerment and confidence because I was exercising the control and agency I had in my life. We brainstormed ideas and decided things like disc golf, poker tournaments, and even choosing where I want to go for a walk would be a great start.

As I reviewed my notes, I needed to confirm the key insight. "Do you honestly think if I did what I truly wanted, there would be people who would love, encourage, and validate me doing that?"

She was strongly confident. "I really do. Do you think Tracy loves you because of who you are or what you do?" Because of who I am. "How about your kids? And your mom?" Who I am.

"They love you whether you are doing what they think is right or not, and most likely you are the only one judging whether what you are doing is right or not. They will love you no matter what, and they are more concerned with you being happy. They will see you are happy when you choose and act on the right things for *you*; the things you love and that bring you a sense of fulfillment. That's likely what Tracy means when she says she wants to see you happy."

We both knew she was landing punch after punch as she went for the knockout. "You are one of the most eclectic, multi-passionate people I have ever met. You are strong, smart, charismatic, kind, funny, and inclusive. With all the things you have done, have you ever had a problem finding people to join you, support you, and encourage you?"

I let the question sink in, kind of hoping I could think of an example. "No, there have always been people who showed up and were supportive and encouraging."

"Exactly. And no matter what you do going forward, people will emerge. They might not be who you expect, and you might lose some current people, but new ones will be there. You will always have people who validate you and what you do, especially if you are doing what *you* are passionate about and what you want to do."

I simulated holding a microphone and letting it drop to the ground. "Thank you for this."

A new thought entered, and I needed to get her perspectives because we were down to the last fifteen minutes of our time together. "What about the stuff I'm doing right now that I don't like, or the people I don't really want in my life? Can I just quit stuff? Can I break off relationships I don't think are healthy?"

"What do you think?" She was a master of answering a question with a question.

"Well, it seems like it would be hard, but I suppose it's up to me."

"It is completely up to you, Steve." She started moving into that stern, confident posture. "This is your life, no one else's. You have the right to do what makes you happy with people who support you on that journey. You also have the right to stop doing what doesn't make you happy and move on from people who don't support you in the way you need. I'm not going to tell you what to do or not do. I'm not going to give you permission to do those things, because you have the agency to be empowered to give yourself permission to do those things if that's what you want to do."

I felt the need to take a deep breath. The long inhale brought me back to those first days of struggling when I'd leave the office to walk and breathe. Logically I knew she was right, but did I have the confidence to give myself permission to take control of my life like that? If I separated myself from people who weren't good for me, would the right people truly stick with me, or would others take their place? Fears abounded as I wondered what all this truly meant in my life in real time.

The conversations with my therapist stayed on my mind. Her message, "This is your life," was not only written at the top of my notebook but also trapped in my thoughts as a constant reminder.

While I wanted to heal this part of my life, I had too many amazing relationships to start completely fresh. I thought it was a big enough challenge to try and identify the life I really wanted after forty-eight years of accepting defaults, meeting expectations, and trying to accomplish all the things I "should" accomplish. Even with this newfound sense of empowerment and agency about being in control of my own life, I would have to try making choices that were right for me and let go of doing things the "right" way because now I could see there was no right way, only my way, which paved my road ahead through the power of choice.

This challenge might always be with me, but I was excited about the potential of moving in the direction that was right for me, even if it was unright in the eyes of others.

The first big unright decision I made was to work for myself. This felt daunting while also exciting. I saw it as an opportunity to start working more on my terms by choosing the projects and the people I worked for and with. But this decision didn't just affect me. I would keep an open dialogue with those who were close to me so I could reestablish their needs based on my choices. I knew Tracy was an excellent communicator, so I was lucky to have this foundational support, and I trusted there was no accident in my choosing her to be my partner in life and now for greater growth.

I knew being an entrepreneur was the right first step. I also knew I had the work ethic, creativity, and determination to give it my all. My therapist helped me understand if things weren't working, I could always make new choices that changed my experience. I could seek those I trusted as sounding boards for my ideas. I knew there was always support to turn to.

My second step was to release the expectations and "shoulds" from well-meaning friends and colleagues who encouraged me to go back to being an actuary; to not scrap my education and experience when the marketplace was starving for people with my capabilities. These might not be the right people for this delicate next stage of my journey.

There was a financial reality to working on my own. I needed to make money. Tracy had benefits through her job, which was a help, but I still needed to fill an income gap. We were both taking a risk in my choice, but we also believed in my ability to succeed, and that made it worth it. I believed financial security would come. It always had in the past, and like my therapist said, I had all the right things inside to succeed.

As we closed out 2018, I made a single public New Year's resolution: to still be working for myself at the end of the year. The other resolution, which I didn't share publicly, was that I wanted to move closer to understanding and living the life I truly wanted.

For the next two years I was able to scrape enough income together to keep working for myself. In my mind I still worried about making enough for the life I'd worked so hard to build before. As part of my business, I started looking to do some paid speaking and had secured ten paid events prior to COVID-19, which put a temporary end to in-person events. All ten speaking engagements were canceled. I was able to pivot and add more consulting contracts supporting other small business owners trying to navigate the pandemic. All of this was enough to get me through 2020, which made me think I might just make it on my own, even if I was doing the unright thing.

The business was still not flourishing by the middle of 2021, and it was starting to become a grind. My focus was split in so many ways, just trying to make enough money from each place that, collectively, we could make ends meet. I was feeling the practical impacts of doing my unright thing and understanding why leaving the security of a corporate career can be so difficult. But I reminded myself I didn't leave a career because I hated the job or the people. I left because I needed to figure out who I am, what I enjoy, and how I can live free from my addiction to external validation.

But in my quest to make a buck on my own, I felt myself falling back into the trap of doing what I should do or what others expected of me, rather than first pursuing what I would really love to do. Every coaching and consulting contract I wasn't very excited about but agreed to do anyway was sucking the life out of me. I would rather get a nine-to-five job than deal with some of those clients.

I started wondering if I was capable of being happy while earning an income. But I remembered some of the early days in my career, and more recently how much I loved officiating small weddings. I loved hearing the story of how couples met or their life today and then being part of their big day. And as live events started happening again, I had more opportunities to share my thoughts through speaking, typically for free, but I loved everything about it.

However, free speaking events and small weddings were not going to be enough income. As we neared the end of 2021, I was at a financial crossroads. Either I had to suck it up and do more of the coaching and consulting I didn't enjoy, go back to the corporate world, or go all-in with one more attempt to build my own business doing something I loved. I gave myself to the end of the year to make it happen, or it was back to a real job.

That would be my last attempt, and I told Tracy that. This time, I was not going to strategize about what the world needed or study how everyone else was doing things. I decided to make this last attempt on my terms, starting with what made me truly happy and come alive, and see what I could create when I started there.

The choice was obvious to pursue becoming a professional speaker in a way that allowed me to unleash the full fury of whatever creativity remained after suppressing it for decades, having given way to math, analytical problem solving, and leadership. Certainly I got nervous, but every time I spoke from a stage, emceed an event, or was interviewed on a podcast, I felt like I was in my element. And, for what it's worth, I thought I had what it took.

I'm a bit of a unicorn as a former actuary who can talk with others, or from a stage, without staring at my shoes. I have amazing stories from all my life experiences, which I could certainly use to provide insights in compelling ways. And my joke-telling, jingle-singing, parody-writing, creative self is maybe still in there.

Even if I could be comfortable enough to let my creativity and experiences come through on stage, I caught myself wondering if that was the right way to become a speaker or if meeting planners and speakers' bureaus would welcome that approach. I watched a few videos of professional speakers, and I realized, almost instantly, that creative use of humor and story was not only okay but seemed to be what the best in the business were doing. I forgave myself for my quick relapse into needing validation as I planned my strategy.

I started infiltrating speaking groups and reaching out to those I really enjoyed, asking if they wanted to be on this speaking journey together. And my therapist was right! New people had taken the place of the old, and they validated and encouraged me, but somehow it felt even more true. The biggest change was that I validated me. Re-listening to talks I had delivered or podcasts I had been a guest on, I liked who I was, and I knew I was doing what was best for me. It might have been the unright thing in the eyes of some of my former colleagues, managers, pastors, and business partners.

It might have even been the unright thing for some of my family and friends.

But here's the thing. It was the right thing for me.

By the end of 2021, I rebranded myself as "The Safari Dude" and my business as The Safari Way. I have been on several African safaris, so I could share fun stories, but this also had the potential to be a creative and differentiating brand. I did have a few coaching clients but focused on becoming a leadership speaker. My work experience included studying the data about what motivates employee behavior, so I paired that with my decades of leadership experience in corporate, nonprofit, and small business settings to become a leadership speaker. I delighted audiences with stories from safaris and how they could build powerful teams, or what I call getting the "right peeps in the Jeep." Just for fun, I sprinkled in a few ideas about how we could approach our life, work, and leadership like an African safari, sharing a quote from Helen Keller, "Life is either an epic adventure, or nothing at all."

But a funny thing happened on the way to becoming a leadership speaker. The greatest engagement and feedback were coming from those who were longing to live their life more like an epic adventure. Sometimes they even cried, sharing, "This is the piece I've been missing." Their realization paralleled my own. I always thought about my African safaris like epic adventures, which they were, and the rest of my life like the stuff that happened between adventures; the stuff I had to do while waiting for the next experience. What if I viewed my entire life as an epic adventure? The very nature of life is filled with ups and downs, highs and lows, knowns and unknowns. This is the human experience, and the more I can embrace it, the more I can embrace the very idea of my life being epic, then the more engaged and happier I can become within my adventure.

The Safari Way has become a movement. It's the driving force for how we approach our experience in this world. It's a perspective we can understand and apply in our lives. With every story of transformation others have shared with me because of The Safari Way, my confidence grows, my quirky authentic-self shines, and my creativity and humor come forward. My message highlights what I hold as most important: wanting to see community over top-down leadership, personal engagement over automation, and most importantly, humility instead of arrogance.

By the end of 2021, I was fully committed to pursuing what I loved and being around those who could support and contribute to the newfound vision for my life. I removed myself from several situations, groups, and commitments. Some of these were emotionally difficult, but none of them were as painful as I initially thought. In all my caring about what people thought about me, I realized they weren't thinking about me as much as I assumed they were. I became more discerning on how much time I spent with certain people and groups.

So here I am, late in 2023, reflecting on the past fifty-three years. The past two years have still been a grind, working weekends and late nights, doing what I could to make ends meet. A few times I've needed to turn over rocks and call in favors to trade hours for dollars, but I am more encouraged now than I have been in a long, long time. After no paid speaking events in 2021, my new brand generated seven paid events in 2022 and twenty-one so far this year with several already booked, months in advance, for next year.

The feedback has been outstanding, and yes, the validation is still something I crave. But the contrast is remarkable. The positive feedback I get is not about how smart or productive I am, but it's about my authenticity. Although I work hard on my content and my craft, people like me for who I am, not for what I produce. Audience members want to stay connected because of my passion for living life like an epic adventure and doing the unright thing, not because they think I can lead their division, solve their problem, or create for them an amazing spreadsheet tool.

Being validated for my authenticity causes me to become even more authentic in how I prepare and deliver talks. I am having far more fun with the audiences, being completely comfortable sharing my raw emotions, funny stories, and yeah, even my creativity. Through speaking, I feel emotions I haven't felt for more than forty years, going all the way back to the couch on the farm and "Weird Al" Yankovic. I feel free during my talks, sometimes singing a phrase of a song that's relevant to a story I am telling. Recently I even wrote and performed publicly my first parody in more than forty years, "The Grain Gambler," a spoof of Kenny Rogers's famous song, "The Gambler."

My time on stage is the closest I have felt to who I was when I was younger and who I think I was born to be for all these lost years. I have greater confidence and feel empowered to keep moving in the direction of my dreams. I am hanging out with people who have the energy and perspective I'm looking for.

This is my life. This is my safari. This is my adventure. I have the agency and permission to choose my experience.

I choose creativity, fun, compassion, and kindness.

My name is Steve Fredlund, and I am The Safari Dude, embracing the adventure of life and helping as many others as possible who are interested do the same. It's hard to imagine a more unright thing to do for an actuary than becoming a motivational speaker, but this is who I am. In reflecting on my early life of writing parodies and being part of a passionate community like college football, I was The Safari Dude way back then. But The Safari Dude was covered up by layer after layer of defaults, expectations, and "shoulds," locked in the good life trap by his addiction to validation.

This book is my coming out party; my celebration of two years operating with awareness of my needs and freeing myself from my dependence on external validation. It may always be part of my life, but with the help of the right peeps in my Jeep, it's something I am overcoming. I am no longer who I "should" be. Steve Fredlund is truly The Safari Dude, just like Clark Kent is truly Superman. If comparing myself to Superman seems like the unright thing to do to you, I'm not sorry. I'm going to do it anyway because it is right for me!

CHAPTER 13:

AS OF TODAY

———

Today is October 25, 2023, as I write this final chapter of the book, but not my life.

For nine months I was writing this book as a how-to manual. In fact, the subtitle initially was going to be, "How to Recognize and Escape the Good Life Trap." I conducted many interviews and did hundreds of hours of research, creating citations for every study I would reference. My plan was to explain, scientifically and through the experiences of others, how trying to do everything right creates a good life for us, which ultimately becomes a trap that is hard to escape. I had hundreds of pages written with more than seventy-five citations from my research.

It was a good book, but it wasn't *my* book. I had been steered that direction by some well-intentioned experts, and wanting validation and to do the right thing, I proceeded down that path. It was exhausting, and I hated almost every minute of it, yet I persisted and had about 90 percent done when I encountered Anne, someone who gave me the freedom to write the book I really had in my heart. That is why you are reading a memoir rather than a self-help manual, because I am not an expert. I'm just a guy on a journey of wanting to be happier, who wants to explain his story to those who aren't aware of it, in hopes it will help others find the courage to do the unright thing in their lives.

I am sitting in the lobby of the Ramkota Hotel in Sioux Falls, South Dakota. I have just finished delivering my signature keynote, "The Safari Way to Greater Happiness," to a state-wide group of deputy clerks. I am looking through my emails to see if I have any other last-minute feedback to include before I press "send" and deliver the final version of my manuscript for the final stages of editing and publication. I know the book is not perfect, but it reflects my heart and my journey. A more experienced author would have connected the dots more expertly and drawn the readers to a greater understanding of the situation and my thought process. Maybe the right thing to do would have been to hire a ghost writer so everything was perfect, but I did the unright thing and decided to write my book from my heart with my words.

The most unright thing most of us can do is to live our lives authentically as ourselves, pruning the weeds that stunt our growth and seeking the people who will be the sun, soil, and water we need to fully flourish. For me, this required a job change away from something I was afraid to admit I didn't like and into something that seemed like a natural fit with who I was forty years earlier. Not all of us need a job change to do the unright thing and live our lives more authentically. We might just need a good friend or therapist, some creative brainstorming, and a little bit of courage.

And for those of you who need external validation as much as I did, let that become a byproduct of living your life with authenticity and passion rather than the validation becoming your primary pursuit. When we live our passion, people are drawn to us because the world is hungry for people of authenticity and passion.

So, there you have it, the last few words of encouragement I want to share. But I want you to know one more thing.

Yesterday I purchased a ticket to the November 18 college football game between my beloved Minnesota Gophers and the mighty Ohio State Buckeyes. The game is at Ohio Stadium, but us true fans know it as "the horseshoe," or simply "the shoe."

One ticket: Section 17A, Row 22, Seat 3.

I considered asking a buddy to go with me, or maybe Stacey, Brian, Chris, Jeff, or Simon. But this is a journey I need to take alone, at least for the first game. There will be raw emotion. There will be toasts made to Grandma and Grandpa Rice and their couch, to Uncle Steve, to Uncle Donn, and to Ray Christensen. Perhaps I will even pack one of my old stats notebooks.

Since a little boy adjusting the TV antenna on a Saturday morning at the farm, I have dreamed about this experience. I could have gone to a large university like Ohio State, or I certainly could have gone to a game like this anytime throughout my adulthood, but something has held me back, likely because it has never seemed like the right thing to do.

Well, cue the marching band. I'm off to do the unright thing.

ACKNOWLEDGMENTS

Thank you to Tracy, my fabulous wife. You have given me a lifelong example of unconditional validation. Your love has been my anchor, keeping me grounded with confidence and happiness during my stormy periods. You have always believed in me, even when I didn't believe in myself, and you continue to remind me I have value beyond what I accomplish. And yes, even if I had gone to TCU, I believe we would have still been together and built this wonderful life.

Thank you to Christopher, Ryan, and Annie. It is an honor to be your father. You have always made me feel like I'm more than just a dad; that you genuinely like hanging out with me. My dream when I became a father was that my children would still want to visit me once they were grown. Thank you for making that dream a reality and for letting me occasionally win Catan.

Thank you to Brian Swedeen, Doug Bearrood, Jeff Fluguear, Pete Troolin, and Stacey and Greta Nelson, my closest and longest-standing friends. You have known me through many seasons of my life, trying to keep up with whatever new thing I was doing but never wavering in your support and encouragement. Your questions, affirmation, and laughter through the years have meant more than any of you will ever realize, grounding me in believing that maybe, just maybe, I am okay after all.

Thank you to the rest of my family and friends with whom I have shared this epic adventure of life. We have shared beautiful moments laughing, playing, studying, working, solving, researching, strategizing, traveling, singing, dreaming, crying, worshiping, deconstructing, and just being together. With the new Steve ready to do more of what I love, don't be surprised if you hear from me soon!

Thank you to my fellow speakers, specifically Simon Anderson, Lena Scullard, Ari Gunzburg, David Shar, Jon Lokhorst, and Jason Hunt. You have become my mentors, friends, and colleagues, always willing to answer my questions and encouraging me to bring my authentic self to the stage.

Thank you to those who read some of the chapters of my draft, providing helpful feedback. Special thanks to those who were able to give feedback on the entire manuscript: Chris Janssen, Ellen Lance, Karl Anderson, Michelle Koch, Simon Anderson, Stev Stegner, and Tracy Fredlund. A special shout-out to Amy Vasterling, who not only provided feedback on the entire book but went way above and beyond in the final days to help make the final version as good as possible.

Thank you to Eric Koester for helping me believe in this project, including the initial brainstorming around the concept. Thank you to the entire team at Manuscripts,

LLC for helping every step on the way, with a special shout out to Anne Kelley for understanding this book needed to be a memoir and then helping me make it happen under extremely tight deadlines.

Finally, a massive thank you to everyone who pre-ordered *Do the Unright Thing* and became part of my author community: Angela Irwin, Annie Tutt, Blake Bohn, Bob Schlichte, Brian Swedeen, Brian Morey, Bryant Nelson, Chris Jones, Chris Gorton, Chris Janssen, Chris Nelson, Clint and Michelle Lundeen, Danny Schneider, David Shar, Doug Drabek, Doug Bearrood, Ellen Siewert, Ellen Lance, Eric Koester, Fred Nolan, Gabe Flynn, Heidi Holkestad, Jack L'Heureux, Jake Mason, Jason Doan, Jason Hunt, Jean and Joe Crocker, Jeff Little, Jim Gibson, John Lemieux, Jon Lokhorst, Karl Anderson, Keith Brandt, Kelly Bretz, Kevin Kelzenberg, Larry Fredlund, Larry and Vicki Ostrom, Lars Leafblad, Laura Smith, Lisa Archambeau and MJ Masters, Mary Brooks, Michelle Koch, Michelle Massman, Nate and Gina Rudolph, Neil Henke, Peter and LeAnne Troolin, Phani Iruku, Ray Queener, Rebecca Bates, Rob Delaney, Ross Bowen, Ryan Fredlund, Scott Nelson, Shane and Heidi Buff, Simon Anderson, Stacey and Greta Nelson, Stev Stegner, Tim Nelson, Timery and JoJo Spencer, Tracy Fredlund, Tracy Schreifels, Tricia Kreie, and Trond Vidar Stensby.